2nd Edition

THE HOUSE OF YOU:

5 WORKFORCE PREPARATION TIPS FOR A SUCCESSFUL CAREER

By
Justin Alan Hayes, MBA

ISBN-13: 9780578438931
CreateSpace Independent Publishing Platform, North Charleston, SC

1st Edition Printing May 2017

2nd Edition Printing January 2019

For quantity sales, please contact the author at
https://www.thehouseofyou.com

For all those who have taught me
to continue to chase my dreams.

CONTENTS

INTRODUCTION

Welcome to THE HOUSE OF YOU. The rapid evolution of technology coupled with companies downsizing and in turn operating in a lean manner (doing more with less employees), has led to a more competitive job market. The days of simply applying to a position on a company's website and receiving a job offer (after the screening and interview process) are gone and will not return. For example, it was common not too long ago to have secured several job offers prior to your college graduation. In fact, my own sister who is 4 years older than I am was one of those lucky people. Today, it is as important as ever to not only acquire an education in a growing field and build an easy-to-read resume for human resources (HR) and associated hiring managers, but to market yourself to your potential employer at each touch point (resume, LinkedIn, interview dress, confident communication, business cards, etc.), including an up to date portfolio with samples of your work from previous professional or volunteer relevant roles or from key class projects completed. This is of extreme importance because you are not the only person applying and interviewing for a position, a position whether right or wrong that you will be compared to your competition in every conceivable way.

You may be thinking to yourself, "Hey I am a college student, so shouldn't the fact I am earning an education in a growing field be enough to be hired?" In very rare instances, yes, but if you are earning a marketing degree and apply for a position requiring a marketing degree, you have to assume that you are not the only person interested in the position who has earned a marketing degree. There are thousands of colleges and universities in the United States of America alone, with many offering similar degrees, so it would be unwise to think you should be offered the position on education alone. What do you need to do in order to have the best shot at the positions you apply to? You need to find the distinguishing characteristics that set you apart from other job applicants. While many of the job applicants for a position may have the same education you do, many may not have your distinguishing characteristics.

Some ways you can distinguish yourself from other potential job applicants while you are a student and/or job seeker are to lead a class project instead of running the clicker, volunteer in your spare time, or join a school club relevant to your major or Toastmasters to fine-tune your presentation skills. This is by no means an all-inclusive list of all professional- related clubs or the only ways to distinguish yourself, merely a few suggestions to help get you in the right frame of mind. In the end, it is ultimately up to you on how much time and effort you want to put in. If I could turn back the clock I would have spent more time preparing than I did. I just wasn't in the right frame of mind or have the knowledge that I had to find ways to separate myself from other potential job candidates. Potential job candidates that just the other day I was sitting next to in my Market Research class finishing up a group project on a local business. Treat others with respect, but also keep in mind that after your training or school is completed you will be each other's competition.

It is with that in mind through feedback from Dr. Eric Terry at Miami Dade College – Hialeah Campus, I have included additional content in this 2nd Edition that will not only teach you but test you with 5 real world Case Challenges, many years in the making. At the same time a Performance Review Preparation Worksheet can now be found at the end of Chapter 6: HOUSE MAINTENANCE. The inclusion of this new material and additions throughout the following pages now provides a 2019 lense with THE HOUSE OF YOU.

THE HOUSE OF YOU will lay out brick by brick how to get started in your quest to position yourself in the best light for a prospective employer. You will additionally learn what areas in the workforce planning and maintenance are within your control, what areas are outside of your control, and the importance of knowing the difference. THE HOUSE OF YOU also includes activities at the end of many of the chapters to help get you started while the content is still fresh in your mind. I hope you enjoy THE HOUSE OF YOU as much as I enjoyed writing it. My goal is to help you along each step of your career journey primarily with knowledge gained from my fifteen years of education and professional experience.

CHAPTER
ONE

THE BLUEPRINT

To provide you a visual of what we are discussing, this book will reference analogies between your workforce preparation tools and building a house because visuals can sometimes help clarify the process we will be using. So, before we get started, take a minute to think about the home construction process as if you were a builder.

As an owner of construction company, what would happen if you decided to begin construction on a new house without a plan? For starters, you would not know how many materials to purchase. This oversight would lead to either a surplus or a deficit. For example, if you purchased enough supplies for a two-story house when the owner only requested a one-story house, you and your construction company would be left with enough materials for two one-story houses. Since you purchased and paid for the materials for the project, you may want to pass these charges to the brand-new owner of the house for all of the materials even though it was your error. Chances are the new owner would be unwilling to foot the bill for your mismanagement, which may cause you and your construction company to lose money on the project and the new owner to question whether you should build their new home, two things nobody wants when running a business, let alone a small business.

The opposite of this scenario would also put you and your company in a negative light in the eyes of the new home owner due to your lack of planning and preparation. If you started construction on a new home, you would not only want to know the quantity of the materials required, but also each type and color of each material needed. A couple examples would be if the owner wanted a log cabin, and you and your construction company purchased materials best suited to a home with siding, or if you purchased tan siding when the new home owner had requested gray.

Not properly planning, mismanagement of building materials, and poor execution are all scenarios that would not be conducive to any company retaining credibility or longevity for any length of term for their business. We have a responsibility to ourselves and our family to ensure we lay out a blueprint for our professional career just as builders should lay out a blueprint for each house they are contracted to construct.

In the simplest terms, the blueprint for THE HOUSE OF YOU is caring enough to prepare for the workforce, regardless of your chosen field of study or expertise. When you care enough to prepare, whether it be in your personal life or your professional career, you are making a conscious effort to control your own destiny to the greatest extent possible. While controlling your own destiny may only seem possible in a fantasy world, controlling your own destiny in areas where you have control can be a reality. For example, when you woke up today, did you have control over what time your alarm would go off? Did you have control over taking a shower, brushing your teeth, and selecting what outfit you wanted to wear for the day? For most of us the answer is yes; I had control over those areas today as I do almost each and every day. The beauty of these examples is that no matter if you live in Beijing, China or Green Bay, Wisconsin or whether you speak Chinese or English, almost all of us have elements of our lives that we can control to a great extent.

In future chapters, I will mention quite a few areas of your life that are within your control as they relate to you and your professional career, as well as things that are out of your control. I want to convey to you the importance of spending your time and energy on the areas that you can control and not worry about things that are outside of your control. This will help alleviate the stress that comes with worrying about things such as what others will think and say about you both in front of you and behind your back. I want to be clear on this because there have been times over the course of my professional career where I have wondered what individuals think or what they might say or feel about a professional event, such as an interview. What I have found is whether or not I worry or analyze each situation, the outcome of that particular event will come and go; the next day the sun will rise, and a new day will begin. Time does not worry; time only advances, and so should you! Save yourself a lot of needlessly wasted time, energy, and stress by controlling what you can control and not concerning yourself with what you cannot control.

Having a blueprint gives you the laser focus and strength to put your best foot forward, to know what you can do and what might be best suited for someone else, to be prepared when given the opportunity to showcase your talent and skills, and to thrive and exceed all expectations for yourself and your family. We want to be focused builders, builders who plan and exceed expectations, not the hypothetical builder we read about earlier in the chapter. The time has come to advance and get started on our foundation.

CHAPTER
TWO

THE FOUNDATION

G reat job! You just completed your blueprint and have taken the important first step to care about your professional career, so it is now time to implement the blueprint. After the blueprint is finalized, and before any house can be built, the land must be first cleared of any trees, brush, and rocks with a bulldozer that is within the dimensions of the lot and new house. Once the land is cleared, construction can now begin.

The next step in home construction after the land is cleared and leveled is to start digging for the basement, otherwise known as the foundation. The basement is dug, in most cases with a backhoe, in preparation for the concrete block to be laid for the foundation of the house. It only makes sense for a house or physical structure to have a solid foundation before installing the subfloor plywood, etc. If the foundation is not solid, then the safety inspector cannot deem the house safe to move into, and the new home owner would have to wait until the home building code is met before they can safely move in.

Many parallels can be drawn between the construction of a home and setting you up for a successful career in the workforce, no matter what industry you are interested in joining and adding value to. As a new home must have a solid foundation, you also must have a solid foundation. The foundation in THE HOUSE OF YOU includes several elements. First, I will list each element and then I will go into greater detail to flush out the specific details. The foundation in THE HOUSE OF YOU includes constructing and having a fresh cover letter, resume, LinkedIn profile, and clean additional social media platforms such as Facebook, Twitter, Instagram, and Snap Chat.

For starters, it is a good idea to understand or begin to understand your strengths and the areas in which you can add value to an organization. Why? Because knowing and understanding your strengths is a key factor in determining whether you are a fit for a position. It is uncommon for you as a job applicant to be a fit for each and every position a company posts, so it is okay to determine the target positions that you are a fit for so you will not lose precious time searching and applying to positions that are not a fit.

Being a fit for a job opening means that the education and/or skills you have earned and possess match what a job description includes. For example, if you have a marketing degree and enjoyed the marketing you did for projects at school and/or during an internship, a potential position fit might be a job description that includes a requirement for the applicant who has earned a bachelor's degree in marketing and enjoys doing that work on a daily basis. On the other hand, if you have that same marketing background we just discussed and the job description states that the company posting the open position is interested in applicants who enjoy working with numbers and have an accounting degree you would not be a good fit for the open position.
So, what do you look at to guide you on what fields and job openings would be a good fit for you? We want to contain all this pertinent information about your strengths, education, internships, and volunteer experience in the form of a cover letter and resume. It is a good rule of thumb to formulate and complete the resume first and the cover letter second. One of the reasons behind this line of thinking is that the cover letter will be drawing highlights

from your resume. While you will be modifying your cover letter for each position you apply for, your resume will be more static, remaining the same unless you obtain new education, skills, and/or experience to update the resume. For example, you may apply to five unique positions at different companies and will want to include a different cover letter for each position but wish to include the same resume. Additionally, you will want to include company-specific information in your cover letter, such as the company name and physical address (street, city, state, and zip code). You would not want to have the company name and address for position 1 at company A on an application for position 2 at company B, would you? No, you would not.

Also, job postings may seek slightly different skill-sets, and you would want to include your specific skills and experience as they relate to each job posting. For example, position 1 at company A uses terminology such as "negotiation skills" and "deal closing" in the job description. In your cover letter for position 1 you would want to make sure that you include your skills and experiences as they relate to negotiation and deal closing. Position 2 at company B, however, does not use such terminology, and therefore, you would not want to include those skills and experience in your cover letter for that position. This is why it is important to interchange your skills and experience based off of each job posting you choose to apply to.

It may sound like a lot of work to prepare a polished cover letter and resume free of grammatical errors, or you may think the hiring manager should just hire you because you applied. There are several reasons why hiring managers need to see your cover letter and resume along with the other applicants'. First, the cover letter and resume shows your prospective employer what education, skills and experience you are bringing to the table versus other applicants. Your cover letter and resume are two distinct but related methods that are universal tools for applicants, HR, and/or hiring managers to make the call whether or not an applicant is a good fit for the open position.

At this point you may be wondering how to get started on your cover letter and resume. The good news is if you are still in school and/or have already graduated from college and belong to an alumni association, all you need to do is to contact the career services department at your school for their cover letter and resume services. Utilizing career services will help in a couple of ways. First, career services has seen a variety of cover letters and resumes from all fields of study, so they have a great idea of what format to use, what information you should include, and in what order. Secondly, the service is FREE!

The key here is that if you utilize a service that may be a word of mouth recommendation from a friend or family member, you could be looking at spending hundreds of dollars on their services. I know I have! But if you have not or are not planning to go to school, you are still in luck. In that case, you may also want to reach out to a local college or university to see if they would be willing to help you out or if they may have a low-cost alternative. If that route does not come together then I would reach out to your friends and family to see if they may know someone in the human resources (HR) discipline that can help you out.

If all of those avenues turn out to be dead ends, then I would Google "cover letter and resume service." You may also want to add the geographic location that you would like this service to be located near. You may live in North Carolina, but the service with the best reputation may be located in New York. Think about your comfort level in the ability to meet your cover letter and resume specialist face-to-face versus meeting in a virtual setting (telephone, email, Skype, etc.).

One word of caution before paying for any service, I would ask for three references of past clients that you could contact. If the individual is reluctant or unwilling to provide you with this information I would move on (i.e. this could be a potential scam). If you contact those references and see examples of the work this individual completed for them, and it looks like something you would be happy with, then I would move forward in the process.

Another question I would also ask is how long the cover letter and resume process will take (thirty days, three months, etc.) because there may be a job posting you would like to apply to in the next thirty days, and if your cover letter and resume will not be finished for 3 months, that particular time frame will not work for you. Timing is an easy area to overlook, and some individuals are surprised when the cover letter and resume takes longer than they expect. I always err on the side of caution.

My thought process is if I ask for and receive an estimated project completion date, it helps me be proactive with other areas of my job search process. At the conclusion of this chapter I have included a couple of workbook pages that you can fill out and take in when you visit with your career service department, friend that is an HR representative, cover letter and resume specialist, or consulting service that will guide your individual cover letter and resume process.

LinkedIn (www.linkedin.com) is yet another tool that you should maximize to the fullest. LinkedIn is the social media platform for companies and professionals to engage each other regarding company information and news and job openings. If you are not familiar with LinkedIn, it is similar in nature to the Facebook social media platform, but is intended for professionals and provides further information on work experience, skills, and networking groups across all industries. LinkedIn is free to join, but has an available premium upgrade option for a nominal monthly fee. The free version is what I use, but it is up to you if you feel the premium upgrade would be more beneficial to you and your needs.

I am covering LinkedIn at this point because the main objective of creating and maintaining a LinkedIn profile is to compliment your cover letter and resume. You may be asking yourself, "Why can I not just create a cover letter and resume and call it a day?" That is a great question, but as someone who has recruited, hired, and developed professionals, I can attest that the LinkedIn profile is just as important as the cover letter and resume. Another benefit of having a completed LinkedIn profile is that when proactively sourcing for candidates to fill open positions, recruiters use LinkedIn as a source. There are specific tools and solutions available for companies to search, screen, and contact LinkedIn members in an effort to network and find qualified candidates for their positions.

For example, let us assume you apply for a job for which I am the hiring manager. Included in your application submission are your basic contact information, cover letter, and resume. When the job posting closes for applicants to apply, I have received ten applicants (one being you) for the open position. So, what do I do once the position closes? I begin reviewing each of the ten applicants' submitted application, cover letters, resumes, AND their LinkedIn profiles. You may be asking why a hiring manager would do that. The reason I and many other hiring managers utilize LinkedIn is because it is another data point to determine whether or not we want to move a job applicant through the hiring process.

One of the key areas we hiring managers look at with regards to LinkedIn is whether or not an applicant has a profile that is up to date. If the job applicant has a LinkedIn profile that is up to date, the information listed in their profile should be consistent with their cover letter and resume. You would be surprised at how many times the cover letter and resume do not match with an applicant's LinkedIn profile. If you were a hiring manager, what would you be thinking if that happened? You may be thinking, "Is this the same individual that applied for this position? Did they embellish accomplishments on their cover letter and resume, or on the flip side did the applicant embellish their education and/or accomplishments on their LinkedIn profile?"

As an applicant, the last thing you want is to have a hiring manager begin questioning you and your integrity before an interview even takes place. In my experience, one of two things happens if there are inconsistencies. 1) I put this applicant into the PASS pile, or 2) I put the applicant into the MAYBE pile. What is the MAYBE pile? The MAYBE pile is reserved for applicants that have raised questions as to whether they should continue in the hiring process, but have enough attributes I am looking for in the position. Some applicants in the MAYBE pile move forward and some do not. Make sure you do your best to not end up in the MAYBE pile due to a misunderstanding. I will reiterate that at the end of the day you do not want any HR representative and/or hiring managers having questions about your integrity. Would you want to hire an individual that lacks integrity if you were in the shoes of the hiring manager? I know that I do not want to go down that road.

Cover letters, resumes, and LinkedIn profiles are controllable, meaning we are all responsible for creating and modifying the content that is viewable in these tools. Whereas impressions from others about us are uncontrollable, meaning we cannot control anyone other than ourselves. You may not get every job you apply for, but if you limit ambiguity about the things you can control, you will be in a much better position for success in all areas of your life, especially in the workforce!

Building off of the importance of LinkedIn, so too is it important to have clean additional social media platforms, such as Facebook, Twitter, Instagram, and Snap Chat. I will cover this area in two ways: before employment and during employment. Before employment is the time before you become an employee at a company, while during employment is the time while you are a paid employee at a given company. A paid employee at a given company can also be referred to as an active employee.

Having a clean social media presence is another controllable element where you control the information that is projected and viewable to others. As the job market has become more competitive over time, some hiring managers and HR representatives have begun taking an applicant's social media presence into account when considering them for potential employment. I will keep this section brief by stating that it is in your best self-interest to not post anything on social media that you would not be comfortable having a hiring manager and/or HR representative view. This also includes during the time you are an active employee at a company. More than once an employee has gone home after a workday and posted a negative statement about their manager, colleague, or company in general on social media to find themselves coming into work the next day and being told they are no longer an employee of the company.

Once again, control what you can control, and do not expend time, energy, or resources worrying about what you cannot control! Take some time to get started on your foundation with the following Cover Letter and Resume Preparation Worksheet.

Cover Letter and Resume Preparation Worksheet

Primary and secondary education:

_____

_____

_____

Strengths that translate to the workforce:

_____

_____

_____

Technical skills (e.g. project management, data management and analytics, social media experience):

_____

_____

_____

Key projects worked on and deliverables:

_____

_____

_____

Industries of interest:

_____

_____

_____

Internship experience (organization and skills gained (e.g. project management, negotiation, cross functional team management)):

_____

_____

_____

Volunteer experience:

_____

_____

_____

CHAPTER
THREE

THE FIRST FLOOR

O nce the foundation of a house is laid and solidified, we are then able to continue the house construction process with the first floor. We talked about building your foundation in chapter 1 because if you decided the best way to build a house was to start with the first floor instead of the foundation, you would soon find out that there was no solid structure for support, and your house would consequently collapse. Once you have a solid foundation (cover letter, resume, LinkedIn profile, and clean additional social media platforms, such as Facebook, Twitter, Instagram, and Snap Chat) intact, you are now at the point where you can begin the job search process.

Job searching has evolved over the years from mailing your cover letter and resume to a prospective employer to now, in some instances, being able to apply for a position with a couple swipes and taps of a finger on your smart phone. Knowing the ways to apply for a job opening is important since each company can choose their own method and process. So, let us go ahead and jump into some specific job searching criteria, starting with identifying the geographic locations that you would be comfortable working in. I am referring to not only the town/city/state that the employer is located, but also how comfortable you are with the commute time and required methods of transportation.

The term "commute" in its simplest form is the amount of time it takes you to travel to and from a location, whether your method of transportation is one or a combination of the following: a motorcycle, scooter, subway, train, bus, automobile, or airplane. The reason we want to start our job search with the geographic location of the potential employer is because if the furthest you have commuted previously is fifteen minutes each way then you have to determine if you would only be okay with a commute time of fifteen minutes or less, or if you could tolerate a commute of, let's say, an hour each way for a commute totaling two hours.

You may have heard the saying, "time is money." Time is money in this case because, as we will talk about in a later chapter, you will want to ensure that you are being compensated for 1) the time you spend commuting AND 2) the non-monetary loss of time with your family, which is tough to put a specific monetary value on.

You are in a good spot once you determine the geographic locations you would be comfortable working. We then move into the stage of identifying what prospective employers are situated in your pre-determined geographic locations AND the industry they each serve (healthcare, financial services, steel, etc.). This particular task can be completed with an Internet search. Let's say that through your research you have found that there are five employers in the geographic area you selected, with two serving the healthcare industry, two serving the financial services industry, and one serving the steel industry. The industry of the employer is important because a job serves the needs of two specific entities, 1) the employer and 2) you.

So, if you are an employer in the steel industry, one of many characteristics you would be looking for in a job applicant would be whether 1) the applicant has steel industry experience or whether 2) the applicant has taken an interest in the steel industry via a class project or a positive word of mouth recommendation from a friend or family member who works in or has experience in the steel industry. If as a job applicant you do not have steel industry experience or a drive to earn it, you may not be the best fit for that particular company. This is not to say that not having the industry experience of the employer is a bad thing; it just means that the road to earning a job there may take more of a winding approach as opposed to a straight path from point A to point B.

You may be wondering how the employer finds out this information about job applicants. One way the employer obtains this level of information is from the foundation you and the other job applicants built in chapter 1. It is okay to eliminate an employer from your job search based on the industry not being a great fit for you. This gives you the ability to focus your time, energy, and resources on those employers that serve the industries that match your experience and interests.

Once you have identified your ideal geographic areas and the industry that those employers service, it is time to maximize your network (friends, family, former students you had classes with, former teachers, coaches, etc.) to determine if any of these individuals works at, or has worked at, any of the employers you are researching for potential employment.
A quote you may have heard before is "it is not what you know, it is who you know." While this is not a hundred percent correct, the percent of accuracy is rising higher each day. Earning a job is extremely competitive because you may apply for a job that twenty-five other candidates also applied for, but if you are the only candidate who applied that already knows someone who works at that potential employer, you will be one step ahead of those candidates that do not. Even better would be a scenario where your connection is in HR because an HR employee may have additional insights you can glean, such as who the hiring manager is or how many other individuals have applied for the same position.

You can maximize a connection at a possible place of employment by contacting your connection via whichever communication method you are most comfortable with and asking if you can chat either in person, over the phone, or via an audio-visual program such as Skype or FaceTime because you have an interest in learning more about the organization. Through my experience, I have found that people, generally speaking, will take the time to have a discussion with you if you communicate in a polite and respectful manner. One caution is to ensure you make your best effort to not waste yours or your connection's time. If you are meeting for a half hour, do not spend twenty of the thirty minutes catching up and only leave ten minutes to discuss the reason you wanted to meet in the first place.

The topics you plan on discussing should include the company and industry, the connection's position and department at the company, and if you would be a good fit there. If after the discussion, you still feel good about the company and industry, it is then acceptable to ask your connection if it would be appropriate to send your cover letter and resume in case the connection or someone in the department knows of a current open position for which you may be a fit. Now you can start to visualize how having a connection at a potential employer could give you a small leg up on your competition. From here, you may or may not have communication with this connection for a period of time. Either way, it is okay.

Before utilizing a connection (someone you know), make sure you or someone you know and respect has vetted the connection as much as possible, meaning if you know that the connection has had a less than stellar past, you may not want to have that person in your corner during your job search journey. This does not mean to turn away completely, but be clear with the prospective employer that while you do know the connection, you want to be considered for the position based on your own education, skills, and experience, not theirs.

Since you should not stop our job search until you are hired, after you go through the exercise of identifying and establishing communication with your connections at a potential employer, you will want to search and locate them on LinkedIn to add them as connections. Following a connection on LinkedIn means you will see that person's updates in your news feed, which is a function that you can view at your convenience any time you log onto LinkedIn. Just as you will want to add and follow professional connections, you will want to also follow all of the companies you have identified as potential employers. This gives you the opportunity to gain more familiarity with the organization because more and more organizations are now including their mission statements, you can view current job openings, and companies are able to view who is following them. This function of LinkedIn could lead to you being contacted by a recruiter for a job opening. Even if you are not contacted directly by a recruiter from a company you are interested in, as I alluded to earlier, many organizations are now posting their job openings on their LinkedIn page.

Some employers also give you the ability to submit your interest in a job opening by applying directly through a quick apply method that only takes a few seconds and can even be completed from your smart phone. The quick apply feature electronically sends your LinkedIn profile to the recruiter at the organization of choice and gives you the ability to upload your cover letter and resume to the quick apply action message. This is a much more streamlined and efficient process than sending your cover letter and resume through USPS!

Simultaneously you will also want to search for and identify the company websites you are interested in possibly joining to learn more about them, as well as searching and applying for open positions, which are often posted on a company's website. The location of open positions on each company's website may vary, although in many instances there will be a link in the site's navigation titled "Careers," "Career Section," or another variation of those terms. Click on the "Career" link, and you will be automatically directed to that company's career section where open positions, employee recruiting videos, and other career-related information is posted along with the ability to create and maintain a job search profile specific to that company.

Once you have identified the career section of your companies of interest, your next step will be to create your job profile for each and every company you are interested in joining. These profiles can take anywhere from a couple of minutes to more than thirty minutes each, depending on the requirements of that particular organization's HR department. Again, each company can decide whether or not to have a career section on their website, and it is their decision as to the layout, design, and available functions. For the sake of being on the conservative side, when you sit down to create your profiles, make sure you have at least thirty minutes of uninterrupted time available, including silencing your cell phone and powering off your television.

The basic information required in most job profiles is your name and contact information. You will also have the ability to upload your resume and cover letter, geographic preferences, ability to relocate, education, volunteer service, and any professional experience you may already have. There is also an area on most profiles to include website links that may be helpful for the organization to learn more about you as a candidate. This area is where you will want to copy and paste the URL of your LinkedIn profile. See how each area we discuss is building on the previous?

One area that we will cover in a future chapter, but which you may be asked to include in your job profile, is "salary expectations" or "salary requirements." You will want to enter the dollar amount that you are asking for the organization to pay you as an associate per hour or per year (referred to as salary). Money is always a touchy subject. Many of us think we should be paid more than what the free market is willing to pay for our services, so be careful not to price yourself out of a job opportunity because of stubbornness.

Do an internet search for elements you will want to consider and include when deciding what you will ask a company to pay you. Here is what a hypothetical search may look like: "What is the average salary for someone with a finance degree in Los Angeles, CA at Sony?" Many different websites will populate on your screen to filter and choose from. One website I would check out to give you a starting point is Glassdoor (www.glassdoor.com). I do not recommend using this site exclusively in your salary research because some individuals that post their salaries tend to exaggerate high or low, and some companies withhold what information actually gets populated for you to see. The company's withholding of information pertaining to salaries sometimes also relates to the withholding of past/present company employee reviews about company culture, people, and working conditions to name a few. In addition, I would also refer to the career services department at your college or university for a reference point as well.

Make sure that you maximize each job profile you create to the fullest potential. When you set up your job profiles there is usually an option for you to create what is called a job alert. A job alert within a job profile is a tool where you are able to identify your geographic preferences and the department you are interested in (e.g. Los Angeles, CA / Finance). From here you can then set up the frequency that the job alert will send you email updates on the availability of open positions meeting your specific personal criterion. I recommend setting these up for each organization that you have an interest in.

The last area I want to cover in this chapter is similar in nature to the job profile and automated job alert emails but instead this tool aggregates the open positions from all companies that subscribe to their service within your personally selected parameters and sends you an email with all pertinent details (job title, job description, option to apply, etc.). This aggregation tool is offered with LinkedIn as well as Indeed.com and other similar sites. I am only naming the most popular aggregation sites at time of publishing since new aggregation sites are created on an almost daily basis. The LinkedIn aggregation tool creates your job alert with your already established profile and other specific information such as geographic locations, industry, and job type layered on top. Indeed.com does everything LinkedIn does except use your LinkedIn profile.

We have covered a lot of information in this chapter that allows you to get your job search up and running, which I know will be extremely helpful for you at any stage of your professional career. The following Job Search Preparation worksheet gives you an opportunity to document some of the key information that will be helpful in maximizing your job search while it is still fresh in your mind.

Job Search Preparation Worksheet

Preferred geographic locations:

_____

_____

_____

Companies located in preferred geographic locations:

_____

_____

_____

Industries of experience and/or interest:

_____

_____

_____

Connections at companies in preferred geographic locations, industries of experience, or interest (company, name, and contact information for each):

_____

_____

_____

Job profiles created (organization, URL, frequency updated, user ID, user name, and password for each profile):

_____

_____

_____

CHAPTER
FOUR

THE SECOND FLOOR

You are doing great! You have made it to the second floor of THE HOUSE OF YOU where you have advanced to the next stage in the process, an interview for the job you want at the employer you want, and in the geographic location you want! How exciting! By making it to the second floor you have already laid your foundation and finished constructing the first floor. We are now at the point where we want to leverage all the knowledge and activities we just learned in establishing our foundation and first floor. Exciting as this is, we need to look at several topics that will prepare you for when you are contacted by an HR representative or hiring manager communicating their interest in interviewing you for the position you applied to.

The first area we will discuss is what exactly is an interview? Per Wikipedia, an interview is "A conversation where questions are asked and answers are given. In common parlance, the word "interview" refers to a one-on-one conversation with one person acting in the role of the interviewer and the other in the role of the interviewee. The interviewer asks questions, the interviewee responds, with participants taking turns talking."[1]

---

[1] https://en.wikipedia.org/wiki/Interview as stated on November 15, 2016

The interview can take three different forms and may happen at different stages of the recruitment process, depending on their company hiring protocol. The three different forms of interview are: telephone interview, in- person interview, and/or video-conference interview. Having experienced all three types of interviews in my career, I am uniquely positioned to share my insights with you. Let's get started with the first interview type: the phone interview.

The phone interview is an event that is scheduled at a time mutually agreed upon between you and the prospective employer (HR representative and/or hiring manager). My advice is to choose a date, time, and location when you are free and will not be interrupted. The prospective employer does not want to hear a car or train passing by, a TV in the background, or any other disturbance that might take their mind away from the task at hand, which is to identify whether you are going to be a good fit for their organization and the position you have applied to versus other job candidates. While this should register as common sense, it has happened on more than one occasion where an interviewee does not follow this instruction and in turn does not move forward in the interview process. You should also turn your phone to silent and do not turn the vibrate function on because that could also be disturbing for your interviewer. A few ideas of places where you could conduct a phone interview are: a room at your home, a home office, sunroom, basement, or inside of your parked car with the stereo volume turned off.

For the purposes of this chapter, let us now assume you have scheduled your phone interview and are curious as to what would be the best use of your time between the scheduling of the interview and the time when the phone interview takes place. You will want to stay focused on the phone interview task at hand and do several things starting with researching the company that you will be interviewing with. What information are you interested in mining for? From their company website, you want to locate and document company facts such as company sales, number of employees, mission statements, geographic locations, and product lines. Why, do you ask? One question that is almost always asked in any interview type is why you have taken an interest in the organization. You want to be put yourself in a position to state solid fact-based reasoning for why you have taken an interest in a particular organization and not only because you want a job and need the money. This is one way some interviewees slack off and do not prepare for an interview, but not you!

A second action you should take is to study and learn the position description inside and out. Just as interviewers may ask why you have an interest in their organization, another popular question is why you are interested in the specific position you applied to. Having a great sense of the position description will give you the best opportunity for a great response! One word of advice that I will add here is that when you answer any question that an interviewer asks, please make sure to always keep these two things in mind: How will I add value to this organization, and to this position specifically if given the opportunity? And what are the unique characteristics (such as volunteer experience, teaching experience, lead team projects in school, etc.) that I have that other candidates may not have?

The importance of these questions cannot be overstated. In the hyper-competitive job market we find ourselves in, there are more than likely several job applicants for the very same position you applied for! Due to the fact that many candidates may have similar education, skills, and experience, an employer is in search of distinguishing characteristics that set each applicant apart. By preparing and stating your value-add qualities in an interview setting, you have taken the initiative to share why you are the best fitting candidate for the open position. At the end of the day, that is all you can do, and it is something within your control.

Let me be clear here that not every interviewer will ask the question directly. The interviewer may hint at it or may take a different approach and want you to be proactive by showing how hungry you are and why you are the best candidate for the position. I have experienced both situations, being asked why should we (the employer) move you (the candidate) forward in the process and/ or hire you instead of another candidate, and I have proactively volunteered why I am the ideal candidate at the end of the interview when asked if I have any questions or wish to add anything further. The key here is to be ready for both situations because very rarely will an interview go exactly how you envisioned. Practicing and simulating both scenarios ahead of time will prepare you for whichever path the interviewer goes down.

Another action you should take prior to a phone interview is to search LinkedIn for the individuals you will be participating within the phone interview. This gives you the ability to learn more about the individuals you will be speaking with, such as their education, skills, and experience. Who knows, maybe they went to the same school as you or have experience that intrigues you. You have a good idea that the prospective employer is taking the time to learn more about you on your LinkedIn page, so why not flip the script and use it to your advantage?

The day of the phone interview is here. Be confident in who you are, your abilities, and trust that the outcome will be positive, because it will! If for some reason the employer decides not to move forward with you for the open position after the phone interview, you have just gained valuable experience that will undoubtedly help you in future phone interviews. At the end of this chapter you will see a few of the most commonly asked interview questions to help you to start your very own interview preparation. When preparing for an interview, please remember to use the supplied questions at the end of the chapter as guidance and not as though they will be the actual questions you will be asked in an interview.

The in-person interview is a second interview type that in most cases follows the phone interview. The in-person interview may or may not be with the same individuals who conducted the phone interview, so it is in your best interest to ask who the participants will be if your HR representative has not already provided you with this information. In my career, I have had cases where both the phone interview and the in- person interview were with the same individuals, and I have also had instances where the interviewers were different. Nothing is a given, so be sure to do your due diligence so there is one less surprise on interview day.

Even if you have a phone interview and in-person interview with the same individuals at one company, the structure and process may be different at another organization. Each company chooses their respective hiring process that best suits their company and is not required to follow any specific mandate or protocol. My general rule of thumb is to never assume, and to always ask the company HR representative you are working with during the hiring process about what their interview structure is. It may also be helpful to ask the HR representative during the phone interview if the interview structure has not been already shared with you. Knowledge is power, and you can never have enough of either.

Instead of the interview being conducted over the telephone, the in-person interview is a face-to-face one-on- one or one-to-several interview that occurs in an office or conference room setting in the headquarters or satellite office building of the prospective employer. The great thing here is we can apply all of the same preparation tactics that we installed for the phone interview but with a couple of additional tactics. The additional areas of focus for this particular type of interview are personal appearance, arrival time to the in-person interview, interpersonal communication skills execution, and handwriting a thank you to each one of the individuals you interviewed with after the conclusion of the in-person interview.

The personal appearance that you advertise in an interview setting is another element that is within your control. What I can tell you from my experience is that wearing jeans is not acceptable for ANY interview, and it is unacceptable for females to wear a skirt or dress that is less than mid-thigh when seated. I remember one in-person interview that I had where the HR representative stated it was okay to dress casually for the interview. I could have decided to wear jeans and a t-shirt to be comfortable. Instead, I chose to wear a full suit as I detailed earlier in this chapter. An interview is a form of first impression and your opportunity to shine with a prospective employer, not to show off your newly purchased jeans that you would wear to class, or a skirt better suited for the local watering hole.

If you decide to wear cologne or perfume, please apply lightly as a strong smell or application could also distract the interviewer from your conversation, which is not something you want to take a chance on. Just because you think it is the best smelling fragrance in the world does not mean that the interviewers will have the same perspective. The application of a cologne or perfume may sound like it should not matter in an interview setting, but the last thing you want is for the interviewer to start sneezing or coughing in the middle of the interview because of the overpowering fragrance. How embarrassing would that be? It has happened before, and in most cases a candidate is not moved forward in the hiring process.

If you are a male, you will want to wear a full navy suit with a white or blue dress shirt, a conservative color and style of tie (no bright colors or distracting patterns as that could take the attention of the interviewer away from your discussion), and black dress shoes. Females are recommended to wear a conservative navy blue pant suit, simple jewelry (no large hoop earrings or bedazzled necklaces or bracelets as this could distract an interviewer), and a comfortable type of shoe because you may find yourself taking a tour of the office and/or plant during your in-person interview.

Right now you may be thinking, "Hey, you are a male, so how do you know what is acceptable for a female to wear to a job interview?" For one, my recommendations stem from feedback I have received from my significant other, who is a female in management, and two, I have had similar experiences in my time interviewing prospective candidates. What I have here is only a recommendation of a good rule of thumb to follow regarding acceptable interview attire. I suggest that you take some time beforehand to research the specific field you are interviewing in because the field you are interviewing in may have similar or different standards and expectations for interviewee attire.

For perspective, I want to put you in the shoes of the HR representative and hiring manager and ask you a couple questions. On optics and appearance alone, would you have a more favorable feeling towards a male job candidate who came to the interview in faded jeans with holes in them, a white t-shirt, and a pair of bright red tennis shoes who also smelled like he poured an entire bottle of cologne on right before the interview OR a job candidate as I have described above wearing a full navy suit with a white or blue dress shirt, a conservative color and style of tie, and black dress shoes, not smelling like they poured a whole bottle of cologne on? The latter would be the correct choice.

You may think, "But what if the HR representative explicitly tells me that I can wear whatever I want to the job interview?" That is a fair question, but the HR representative communicating that it is okay to wear what you want to the interview could mean a couple of things. One, it could mean that the HR representative wants to test your judgment on your choice of interview attire, or two, it may be okay to not wear a full suit and tie because maybe the open position you are interviewing is for a management position at a manufacturing plant, where the in-person interview will also be held. Remember to ask the HR representative and research the field you will be interviewing in. Between those two pieces of information, you will be in great shape as to the proper interview attire for your given field.

Throughout my career, I have had experience in both scenarios, but I have always opted for the full suit and tie because regardless of the situation I knew that if all things were equal for all job candidates interviewing for the position, that being conservative by wearing a full suit and tie might just result in earning a job offer. How does what you wear to an interview flow into the interview itself? It has been my experience that if you look good, you feel good, and if you feel good, you do good. Lastly, another good way to look at this situation is that the job interview is one important event in your life that it is better to be overdressed rather than under dressed for. I have never left an interview thinking, "Wow, this candidate was over dressed." But I have left an interview thinking, "Wow, this candidate was under dressed for the occasion."

Be smart, do your research, and ask questions if you are unsure what to wear.

The time in which you arrive to an interview is another important area to cover. Showing up too early could cause the interviewer to have to adjust their schedule to accommodate you. On the other hand, showing up late to an interview gives the interviewer a bad vibe because that brings into question whether or not you will also show up late to work. In both cases, the controllable actions you take could sway the interviewer's opinion of you before the interview even begins! We do not want that, so I recommend that you arrive to the parking lot of the employer twenty to thirty minutes prior to the time the interview is scheduled to start.

Remember, I said arrive early to the parking lot and not to the front desk receptionist! One reason for this recommendation is that you do not have to worry about being late because you are already parked and on-site. It also gives you a chance to spend a couple of extra minutes reviewing your resume, position description, questions to ask, and lastly to compose yourself by taking a few deep breaths to calm yourself down if you feel the onset of nervousness before entering the interview. Ten minutes prior to the scheduled start time of the interview, gather your portfolio, turn your phone off, and proceed to confidently walk to the entrance you have been instructed to enter by the HR representative you have been working with (some entrances are for employees only and others are for visitors, which you are at this time).

This is a great lead in to maximizing your interviewing interpersonal skills starting from the instant you walk through the front door of the employer you are interviewing with. Confidently walk up to the receptionist, make eye contact with a smile on your face, and say something to the effect of, "Good morning, my name is Justin Hayes, and I am here to meet with John Smith and Maria Rodriguez at 10:00 AM."

The receptionist is not who you are interviewing with, so why do you have to exhibit confidence and polite pleasantries? The reason is quite simple; HR representatives and hiring managers alike want to incorporate as much information about you when making the decision of whether or not to move you forward in the hiring process. So, it makes a lot of sense for the HR representatives and hiring managers to solicit the feedback from everyone that had an interaction with you that day. Not only does this help the prospective employer, it also helps you set the tone for the discussions you are able to embark on once the in-person face-to-face formally begins.

The receptionist may tell you to take a seat while they notify your interviewers that you have arrived. Having arrived in the lobby five to seven minutes earlier than the interview start time is the sweet spot. A minute here or there will not make it or break it, but walking into the lobby thirty minutes early or ten minutes late could. If circumstances will affect your arrival time causing you to be late, communicate with the HR representative that you apologize, but due to this unforeseen circumstance you will be late and arriving at X time. The prospective employer will be much more forgiving in this case than if you do not communicate with them and merely show up late with no advance warning. How you handle a situation like this directly relates to valuing your personal responsibility to treat others how you would want to be treated, especially in a manner that may lead to your employment.

Once the interviewers come to the lobby to receive you, have a smile on your face, make eye contact, and greet each interviewer. Shake each of their hands and thank them for the opportunity to discuss the position. After you walk from the lobby to the office or conference room where the interview will be taking place, make yourself comfortable because you will most likely be in the same location for a period of time (thirty minutes to several hours). If additional interviewers enter the office or conference room, you should make eye contact, stand up, and greet each interviewer. Shake each of their hands and again thank them for the opportunity to discuss the position, and hand each a fresh copy of your resume and your business card.

You may be thinking to yourself, "Hey, I am a college student, so how would I have a business card to hand out at an interview?" That is a great question! Whether you are a college student or not, I suggest that you always have business cards in the event of an interview or a networking function. Creating a business card is a straight forward process that is another self-marketing tool to promote you and your personal brand! You can create a business card at your local Staples, Office Max, or similar place of business with assistance from one of their employees. You can choose to have your business cards printed the same day in store or you can create your business cards online and pickup in store if you do not have a time-sensitive interview or networking function within the lead time window for the production of your business cards.

The key information you will want to include on your business card is your name, title (if you are a student you would simply put "student" in that area), and your contact information (email address, LinkedIn URL, Twitter handle, etc.). The cost for creating and printing a quantity of fifty business cards is about what you would pay for a pizza ($15–$20). The last point about business cards is that by distributing your business card to your interviewers it gives you an opportunity to leave something behind that they can refer back to for your consideration in the recruitment process, which may be a distinguishing characteristic separating you from other candidates.

Once the interview begins, sit up straight, and maintain a smile and eye contact with each interviewer. Try not to look up or down or away from the interviewers, and try not to fidget by tapping your feet, rocking back and forth in chair, or tapping a pen on the table. Looking away gives the interviewer the appearance that you are not prepared with an answer and/or may be untruthful in your responses. On the other hand, fidgeting can distract the interviewers, which is something you want to avoid at all costs. Do not worry; everyone gets nervous in an interview! The key here is to have practiced mock interviews with your friends or family enough prior to your interview so that you feel as confident and comfortable as possible.

Mock interviews role play your friends or family members as the interviewers asking the questions to you, the interviewee. If you are uncomfortable mock interviewing with your friends or family, another avenue is available to you.

Mock interviewing is often offered by the career services department of your school, which allows you the chance to mock interview with a member of the career services department. Please consider taking advantage of this service, or ask one of your teachers more about it as they may also be able to help you practice interview preparation. Practice puts you in a prime position to succeed. I cannot think of another workforce preparation area that is more important than for you to practice interviewing for a position that will help you achieve your financial goals and support you and your family.

You took advantage of mock interviews in your own way and are leaving the in-person interview feeling great. You knocked it out of the park because of your preparation and execution, now what? Either at the beginning or end of the interview each interviewer should have handed you one of their business cards with all of their contact information. If they did not have a business card, do not be shy; ask them for their email and make a note of their name and its spelling, their title, and the business address.

Having contact information for each interviewer gives you the opportunity to complete the important next step, sending each interviewer a handwritten thank you note. A handwritten thank you will show the interviewers that you are grateful for the opportunity to meet with them to discuss the position at hand, why you are the best candidate for the position (three bullet points that you shared in the interview), and open yourself up to answering any additional questions your interviewers may have.

The handwritten thank you should be sent through the mail either on the same day of your interview or at the latest the morning after. Timing is critical in this case because you do not know when the interviewers will be making a decision on the position, so you want to make sure they see your thank you note at the earliest time possible after the interview takes place. You can also send a thank you email to each interviewer, which I also recommend. I recommend sending a thank you email as well because you do not have to wait for the United States Postal Service to work their magic. If you do not have access to the internet or email at your home, go to your local library, and they will be able to assist you. By sending a handwritten thank you and an email thank you to each interviewer, you have done all you can at this point. The decision is now in the hands of the hiring manager. You are doing great so far!

The third interview method I will be covering is the video-conference interview. The video-conference interview is gaining in popularity for positions that may be remote in nature (e.g. the business is in one location, such as New York City, NY, and you are working from home in Boston, MA). You may have a video-conference interview from your house via a platform such as Skype or you may be asked to attend an in- person interview with a supplemental video-conference interview with an interviewer in another location, which most closely resembles my experience.

My experience included an in-person interview and a supplemental video-conference interview with a hiring manager located in Milan, Italy, while I was in Houston, TX. My unique experience meant that I not only had to prepare for an in-person interview (proper interview attire for the industry of my prospective employer and be on top of my interviewing interpersonal skills I practiced through mock interviewing), but also for a video-conference interview type where one of my interviewers would be projected on two large projection screens, and I would be projected on a third projection screen in my interviewers' local conference room from a web camera.

In this case I had to focus my attention on whichever interviewer was asking me the question, switching my eye contact between in-person interviewers and a web camera for the interviewer in Italy to see and hear me. The key here is to stay within yourself and not worry about whether you are answering a question for an interviewer that is on the telephone, in-person, or via video-conference. I understand this may seem easy in some instances and can be a balancing act in other instances, but with enough practice and preparation through mock interviewing you can master and excel at any of the three interview types!

On the following page, I have listed some of the most common interview questions for you to gain a familiarity with along with the opportunity to document your responses to prepare you for your interviews. Along with preparing for interview questions that there is a strong likelihood you will be asked in one or more interview settings, I have also listed some popular questions that you should strongly consider asking your interviewers because asking your interviewers questions signals your continued interest in the position and prospective employer.

Popular Interview Questions Preparation Worksheet

How did you become interested in our company and this position?

_____

_____

_____

What are three of your strengths and why?

_____

_____

_____

What are three of your weaknesses or areas in need of improvement, and how are you working to overcome them?

_____

_____

_____

Can you tell me about a time when you faced an obstacle on a project, what the obstacle was, and how you overcame the obstacle to complete the project?

_____

_____

_____

What three words best describe you and why?

_____

_____

_____

Why should we hire you instead of another candidate (i.e. your distinguishing characteristics)?

_____

_____

_____

Where do you see yourself in five years?

_____

_____

_____

Popular Questions to Ask Interviewer Preparation Worksheet

- What is your timeframe for filling this position (e.g. as soon as possible, in the next month, by the end of the quarter or year)?

- What does success look like for a new hire in their first ninety days in the role?

- How did this open position become available (e.g. company restructuring, new position due to company and department growth, promotion of employee previously in position)?

- What is the career path of this position (e.g. Analyst > Sr. Analyst > Manager > Director > Vice President)?

- What other departments within your organization will the individual in this position be interacting with and working closely with?

- What does a day in the life an employee at this company look like for an individual in this position?

- How do you see your organization's growth trajectory over the next five years (e.g. positive, flat, down)?

CHAPTER

FIVE

THE ROOF

You have just received a telephone call from the HR representative that wants to make you an offer for the job you interviewed for. How awesome is that? I remember when I received my first job offer over the telephone. I was happy and felt validated that all the time, energy, and preparation I had undertaken over the years were yielding some fruit in the form of a job offer. Some of us may want to be thanked and congratulated on our preparation in real time, but the fact is that preparation is almost always a thankless act when it happens. It is only after you have spent the time and energy preparing that you will be rewarded. Think about it from a sports perspective, a player may perform great in all his or her practices which in the end only give them the opportunity to play on gameday. If the player performs horribly on gameday, they will not receive positive recognition from co-players, coaches and fans. This is even after the player can point to multiple practices of stellar performances.

It has taken me years to become patient and to understand that preparation leads to successful events, although maybe not at the exact timetable you envisioned. Patience is an important virtue, especially as it relates to the workforce. Additionally, you may have completed the final interview three weeks or a month ago and accepted defeat in terms of getting the position you interviewed for since you have not been contacted by the HR representative regarding the status. I remember thinking that if I did not hear from the HR representative in two weeks after the final in-person interview that company must have already filled the position with another candidate. So, what changed my view on this? In one instance, I completed a final interview in August and did not hear back from the HR representative until October with the job offer. After that experience, I threw all my prior assumptions out the window.

Having had experience on the management side of the hiring process, I have seen many instances where a job offer is not extended due to factors outside the control of the candidate, such as budget constraints, upcoming company or department restructuring, or something as simple as the HR representative is out of the office on vacation or a personal day. Once again, control what you can control, and do not spend time and energy on areas that are outside of your control.

The job offer is what I would like to call the roof of THE HOUSE OF YOU. The reason is simple: You can spend countless hours constructing your house from the clearing of the brush to laying the foundation and building floors one and two, but if you do not set a roof over the house, you will find yourself fighting with the elements of the weather. You may be thinking, "Okay, I am following your line of thinking, but what is the definition of a job offer, and what is included in a job offer?" The Oxford dictionary states that a job offer is "an offer of employment."[2] The job offer can come in a few different forms, including verbally in-person, verbally over the telephone, or via email. While I have known prior colleagues of mine that have received a job offer in person, I have not personally encountered that particular form and thus can not elaborate. The form of job offers I have most often encountered are a combination of receiving the job offer verbally over the telephone and via email. How this usually works is the HR representative, recruiter,

---

2 https://en.oxforddictionaries.com/definition/job_offer as recovered on November 20, 2016

or hiring manager will call you without notice, asking if you have a couple of minutes to talk. Next the HR representative will say that there is exciting news—the hiring manager wishes to extend you an offer for the position you applied to and interviewed for. Next, the HR representative will describe the different elements of the job offer, base salary and variable performance pay, 401(k) plan, health insurance, and relocation assistance if necessary. The elements of job offer are also reviewed in the Case Challenges at the end of this book. Once the HR representative reviews all of the job offer elements with you verbally over the telephone, you will be asked how you feel about the job offer. Regardless of whether you think that the base salary is too low or that the company is not covering relocation expenses when you are being asked to move 1,500 miles, this is not the time to air those concerns. You will be able to discuss all of your questions and/ or concerns after you have had time to review the total job offer package at your convenience with the important people in your life and summarize your feedback and follow-up questions you want clarified by the HR representative. I recommend asking the HR representative when they need an answer to whether you accept the job offer as is or have questions and/or concerns you want to discuss with them. From my experience on the hiring manager side of the equation, I know the hiring manager would like your answer and feedback as soon as possible, but respects the job candidate taking twenty-four to forty-eight hours for consideration and review before making a final decision. After all, if the tables were turned the hiring manager would in most instances not want to provide an answer on the spot, especially with the multiple parts of the job offer to consider. If you receive the job offer on a Friday, instead of responding over the weekend when the HR representative may not be at the office to take your telephone call, I recommend telling the HR representative that you will contact them by close of business (5 pm) the following Monday. I have not encountered an HR representative who would not allow me a period of time to review the job offer, so you do not need to be worried that the company will rescind the job offer if you ask for time to review.

After the HR representative verbally offers you the position over the telephone, they will email you a PDF document with all of the elements of the job offer included. During my first offer over the telephone, I remember thinking I had to write down everything the HR representative was covering for later review before I was told a copy of the job offer would be emailed to me shortly. I exhaled a big sigh of relief at that point! With all of the emotions running through my body, I was sure that I had written an element down incorrectly and thus influenced my decision to accept or start negotiating prematurely. There is no need to feel like you need to write everything down during the initial job offer telephone conversation with your HR representative.

Let us now advance to reviewing the different elements of a job offer in greater detail. The first element of the job offer that you will consider is base salary and variable performance bonus pay. The base salary is the amount of cash you will receive via paper check or direct deposit to your checking account, every two weeks in most cases. Depending on the role and company you receive an offer from, you may be paid monthly or twice a month. The timing of your pay is determined by your employer and not up for negotiation, so be prepared to be flexible. Let us assume that the company you received the job offer from pays their employees biweekly and the base salary offered is $40,000 per year. This mean that each pay the gross amount you would receive before taxes and other line items (401(k), health insurance, and life insurance to name a few)) for your base salary is $1,538.46. You have two things to look at here. One, is the base salary you are being offered competitive in the market for the job function and geographic location of the position? A website like glassdoor.com will give you an idea of some of this information. One word of caution, if you are not satisfied with the base salary in the job offer and intend to discuss with the HR representative after further review, make sure you are stating facts as to why they should offer you a higher base salary. It would not be wise to contact the HR representative stating you would be happy with $50,000 per year without giving facts to back up your negotiating. I remember one of my previous jobs had offered me a base salary that inside I felt was low, but I did not have any specific facts to back up my claim at the time, just a gut feeling. What I did was exactly what I am recommending you to do. I did my research to build my case for countering the job offer. When I next communicated with the HR representative, I stated the base salary I felt was fair along with the facts to back up my claim. Another angle to look at is your comfort level with the base salary. All things being equal, are you able to cover your expenses (house payment, rent, utilities, gas, car insurance, food, etc.) and save a portion of each pay check? This area is something only you can answer, and you will have to crunch the numbers to help guide your decision.

Since we are reviewing the term "salary," it makes sense to explore a little further. Salary, also called an hourly wage, is just a different way to say that the amount of money you would be paid is $19.23 per hour. I am a numbers person, so I like to explore topics by every number angle that I can. You may be a numbers person just like I am, but even if you are not it is still constructive to have the ability to look at things that way if you want to, which is why I broke the pay down in two different ways. Although the salary is based off of an hourly wage, you will not be paid additional money for the number of hours you work over forty hours a work week (Monday through Friday). This can be referred to as an exempt position. For instance, if your hourly wage is $19.23 an hour based off of a forty-hour work week, but you work fifty hours one week, you will not be paid extra for those ten hours. On the other hand, if the offer is presented in a way that calls out the hourly rate, then the position is most likely an hourly non-exempt position, meaning not exempt from overtime. In this case, you would be compensated for the extra hours worked over forty hours each week. Depending on the industry or field, as a recent college graduate you could fall into either one of these categories. This is something to keep in mind because I was not fully aware of this when I began my first job out of college.

In some job positions, there may be a variable or performance bonus portion of your pay as well as the base or fixed salary we just reviewed. The key term here is "variable." Variable, according to the Oxford dictionary is "not consistent or having a fixed pattern; liable to change."[3] While the base salary is consistent and recurring;

---

3 https://en.oxforddictionaries.com/definition/variable as recovered on November 23, 2016

any form of variable pay is not. The non-consistent nature of anything variable is precisely why I recommend that any mathematical calculations you do with estimating expenses and savings revolve around the base salary and not the variable portion of pay. Unfortunately, I have known people who had planned their expenses and savings around both the base salary and the variable portion of their pay, which led them into financial trouble at the times where the variable portion of their pay had not come as expected. My goal here is to do my best to have you not be one of those individuals.

In a job offer, you may be offered a base salary of $40,000 per year with a potential of another five percent in pay, otherwise known as a performance bonus, a form of variable pay. The performance bonus can solely be based off the financial performance of the employer or a combination of your performance and the financial performance of the employer. You can control your performance, but you most likely will not be able to control the overall financial performance of the employer. Additionally, not all job positions have a variable portion of pay attached to their fixed base salary. If the position you are offered does not have a variable portion of pay, but it is something that you have an interest in, and the research you have completed supplements your position, then it is quite fair to broach the topic with the HR representative you are working with. I have learned that the answer will always be no if you do not ask the question, so why not give it a shot and ask?

Another popular element that is often included in a job offer pertains to a 401(k) plan. According to Investopedia, "A 401(k) plan is a qualified employer-established plan to which eligible employees may make salary deferral (salary reduction) contributions on a post-tax and/or pretax basis. Employers offering a 401(k) plan may make matching or non- elective contributions to the plan on behalf of eligible employees and may also add a profit-sharing feature to the plan. Earnings in a 401(k) plan accrue on a tax-deferred basis."[4]

---

[4]http://www.investopedia.com/terms/1/401kplan.asp as recovered on November 23, 2016

In 2019, the maximum you are able to contribute to your 401(k) is $19,000 for the calendar year of January through December. If the base salary of your job offer is $40,000, and you want to contribute the maximum of $19,000 to your 401(k), the percentage you would want to have deposited each pay is 47.5% or $730.77. The HR department at your company will be the best resource to help you navigate the specifics of their 401(k) program.

I have experience with employers that have not only offered a 401(k) for employees (can be referred to as safe-harbor contribution), but also match a portion of the amount you contribute each pay. A company match is usually a static number that does not change throughout the course of the year where they will deposit pre-tax dollars to your account. For example, the employer that has made you an offer of employment may match the first five percent of what you put into your 401(k) at a hundred percent. So, if you have fifteen percent of your salary assigned to your 401(k) each pay that the employer will match the first five percent of the fifteen percent at a hundred percent, meaning that if the first five percent was $5 then the employer would also deposit $5 each pay to your 401(k) account.

This is not a financial book, but it is safe to say that it would be wise to contribute at least up to the amount the employer matches into your 401(k) each pay because it is as close to free money that you will find. It is important to weigh all elements of a 401(k), base salary, and variable pay when determining whether to accept the job offer as is or choosing to negotiate. While I do have experience negotiating base salary and variable pay, I do not have experience in negotiating the amount an employer matches their 401(k) plan because that decision is made by top management annually and then is cascaded throughout the company. Base salary and variable pay attributes, on the other hand, are managed at the department level in the form of a budget and in turn can be negotiated.

For example, if a department has a base salary budget of $41,000 for the open position you are receiving an offer for, that means in theory that if you counter the offer at $45,000, then more than likely the HR representative will only be able to return with an offer of $41,000 no matter how much you counteroffer. Now having said that, there are times where departments will exceed their budget for the allotted position if they are impressed with the job candidate and do not want to lose them to another organization. Once again, this is an area that you cannot control and will not have access to the behind-the-scenes semantics that may be occurring throughout the job offer process by the company. What I wanted to do, however, was to share with you some of the inner workings I have experienced as a hiring manager. Each company, department, and hiring manager has a different philosophy on the topic, so I would focus your time on the things you can control that I have laid out in this book.

Determining if health insurance is offered is an element of the job offer. Understanding the different options and associated premium (cost you pay for health insurance) for each pay is yet another key element that should be well thought out in your decision-making process when a job offer has been made and is under consideration. In a hundred percent of my experience in companies, whether large multi- national billion-dollar organizations or smaller million-dollar organizations, health insurance has been offered. What is the primary difference between the health insurance offered in a large or a small company? Premium costs!

The premium costs deducted from your paycheck in a smaller company will be more than that of a larger organization. Why is that? Generally speaking, large organizations have more employees than smaller organizations. So just as you would expect to receive a lower price point at a bulk warehouse store such as BJ's, Sam's Club, or Costco than from your local grocery store, there is also a discount purchasing health insurance for five thousand employees versus thirty employees.

Relocation assistance concludes the key areas most often included in a job offer, as it is included less often than the other job offer elements we have already reviewed earlier in this chapter.

Relocation assistance when considered in context of a job offer contains certain incentives for individuals to move from the geographic location where they currently reside to the one where the duties of the job are to be performed. For example, an individual may live in Austin, TX but the job the applicant has received an offer for is located in Charlotte, NC, so relocation assistance may be included as an element of the job offer.

The most common elements in a relocation assistance package are cash to cover moving expenses, rent cancellation expenses for those individuals renting, a realtor to assist those who have a house, a realtor to assist in purchasing a house or renting an apartment in or around the geographic area the job duties are to be performed in, and airfare for apartment or house hunting trips if the distance between the old and new geographic area meets distance mileage requirements preselected by the company. Sometimes the new job starts before those individuals who wish to purchase a house in their new location are able to move into their new house. In this case, the relocation assistance package may also include temporary housing in an apartment or company-owned house to bridge that gap between job-start date and move-in date.

There may be more relocation assistance attributes than what you see above, but I wanted to cover the most popular and those that I have direct experience with. Since I have experience in receiving job offers that have included relocation assistance, I am a great resource to be describing this area to you. The cash to cover moving expenses can come in a couple different varieties. The job offer may give the option to move yourself or to enlist assistance from a company that specializes in corporate relocation. If you choose the option to move yourself, then the company would give you a lump sum of cash, generally in your first pay check, to cover your moving expenses, but it would be up to you and your friends or family to execute the move itself, meaning you are in charge of the entire moving process, including gathering, packing, loading, driving to your new destination, and unloading your belongings.

The second option is what I have selected in the past, which is to utilize a company that specializes in corporate relocation. The primary reason I chose this method is because there is already a lot of stress and emotion in moving to a new geographic location and starting a new job, so I did not want the added stress and responsibility of doing it all by myself. With that being said, that was my choice, but everyone is entitled to their own preference and decision. When I chose to contract a company that specializes in corporate relocation, my new employer assigned me a corporate relocation advisor that guided me through all of the required paperwork, set up the packing date, pickup time, driving distance, and delivery of my belongings to my new home. The corporate relocation advisor was also the intermediary between me and the realtor, and was instrumental in helping to managing my relocation expenses such as the house hunting airfare, hotel, and food that were to be reimbursed to me once completed (i.e. service completed with associated receipt). Expenses related to the packing, pickup, drive time, and delivery of my belongings were handled directly by the corporate relocation advisor, which allowed me to follow the schedule instead of creating and following the schedule myself.

The house hunting airfare, hotel, and food associated with the house hunting trip were handled in expense form. Expense form is the method where I made a purchase with my own credit card specifically for my job relocation, and once each house hunting trip was completed, I had to submit copies of all of the receipts for expenses that I had incurred on the house hunting trip as well as fill out an expense report. I then aggregated and sent them via email attachments and mailed hard copies of each of the receipts associated with my relocation to my assigned corporate relocation advisor for reimbursement.

Key information that you will be asked to provide on an expense report are the reason (house hunting trip), what (airfare, food, hotel, etc.), when (date) and the amount spent for each. Expense reports are different at each company, but the criteria I just described have been on almost every expense report that I have filled out, whether for job relocation or company-related travel. If you find yourself in this situation, purchase or reuse an old folder where you can store all of your expense receipts and related documents in one place, so when the time comes to fill out the expense report and send (scan and email or mail receipts to your corporate relocation advisor) in your receipts you know exactly where everything is located.

Some of you may be thinking, just as I did at first, that you will choose to move yourself and pocket the extra cash. I did the math, and in my case, I would have only cleared a couple hundred dollars after expenses, and so I decided it was not worth conducting the move myself. This could have been because I was moving over one thousand miles or because the employer knew the average cost of moving and was not in the business of padding the checkbook of a new hire, and in any event, an extra couple hundred dollars would not change my financial situation dramatically. Maybe you will have a different outcome in terms of the dollars and cents offered in a job relocation package. In any scenario you are presented with, you are free to make the best decision for you at the time the relocation package is offered. I was lucky in that I was offered relocation assistance at different points in my professional career, because the cost to move on my own without relocation assistance could have negated any potential increase in base salary for accepting the job offer.

I will now reiterate that not all jobs offer relocation assistance, and if they do, it could be in a similar fashion to my experience or significantly different since company policies can govern the relocation assistance process how they deem fit. Additionally, in my experience with the method of relocation assistance that I chose to receive there were strings attached to the relocation assistance package itself. Upon my acceptance of the job offer and method of relocation assistance, I had to sign a legal agreement that stated if I left the employer voluntarily before a period of two years had passed from my start date, I had to pay back the full amount of the relocation assistance out of pocket or paycheck deduction. In my situation, the amount I would have owed the company if I breached the legal relocation agreement would have been in the thousands of dollars, which would have been a tough financial hurdle to clear. An agreement like this is protection for the employer against a new hire that may be looking for a free ride to get to a new geographic area without regard for their new job and/or employer.

To close out this chapter, I will review additional screenings that a prospective employer may utilize. A job offer is almost always contingent on passing some form of a drug screen (urine sample or hair follicle). All of my job offer experiences have come conditional on passing a form of a drug screen, regardless of the size of company. This book is not intended to suggest how you should spend your personal time, but instead is intended to provide you with as much information as possible for your workforce success. You are an adult and have the ability to control yourself as it relates to how your actions may impact a prospective employer drug screen. My goal here is simply to help ensure that all of your hard work up until now does not go down the drain because of an uninformed personal decision. In addition to a drug screen, many companies require a background check as well. This usually includes a federal and local criminal check, as well as education and employment verification.

On the following page, I give you the opportunity to reflect on the key elements of the job offer and to give you the ability to compare two separate offers at the same time.

Job Offer Decision Guiding Preparation Worksheet

Offer #1	What Was Offered?	Importance (1 - Very Important, 3 - Neutral, 5 - Not Very Importantl)
Base Salary		
Variable Bonus Performance Pay		
Health Insurance		
401(k) Plan		
401(k) Plan Company Match		
Relocation Assistance		

Offer #2	What Was Offered?	Importance (1 - Very Important, 3 - Neutral, 5 - Not Very Importantl)
Base Salary		
Variable Bonus Performance Pay		
Health Insurance		
401(k) Plan		
401(k) Plan Company Match		
Relocation Assistance		

CHAPTER
SIX

HOUSE MAINTENANCE

Congratulations! You have interviewed for and accepted the job of your dreams. Way to go! While you are excited for good reason, you are not quite finished. Although you now have fully constructed THE HOUSE OF YOU, it may come tumbling down if proper maintenance is not performed. So, let us now begin with a question: What would happen to a house, no matter how beautifully constructed with the best materials or how visually appealing it is with a color scheme that pops if the floors are not swept, food is not cleared from the kitchen after each meal, air filters are not changed or even if the doors are not locked or security system is not engaged when you and/or your family is not home? A house that is not secure or properly maintained will turn from an asset (positive) to a liability (negative) or in other terms, from a blessing to a curse. We do not want your house to be a liability or a curse; we want it to be a great asset and a wonderful blessing!

To be able to achieve the latter, you and your family will need to work equally hard, if not harder, maintaining your house as when you were building it. These analogies are meant to paint you a picture to show that even though you have secured a job (which is one of the goals of this book), you still have to continue to sustain your worth or add value to the organization that you have joined.

Let us consider for a minute that you are the hiring manager. You are in high spirits because as the hiring manager not only did you choose the job candidate that was perfect for the open position, but the job candidate also felt they were a fit for the open position. Fast forward to the day the new hire is scheduled to start at your company. On that first day, the newly minted employee shows up to work at 9 am when it was clearly communicated that 8 am was the work start time. When the new hire finally shows up, they are wearing an untucked Hawaiian shirt, shorts, and a pair of flip flops when it was clearly communicated throughout the interview process that the expected attire was business casual. As the hiring manager, what is running through your head about the new employee? Probably some of the same things that are running through my head and have so in the past, such as curiosity as to why the new hire showed up to work an hour late without contacting you or their HR representative. Another thought may be why would your new direct report show up to work in clothing fit for a beach vacation rather than a pair of dress pants, collared shirt, and dress shoes, which is the expectation for all employees at your organization? All of the hard work this new employee had successfully completed up until now may have been all for not.

I wanted to share this hypothetical new employee with you as an extreme of what not to do. I am aware that new organizations, which some of you may end up employed by, are forming each and every day and that each has their own philosophy on work attire and start time. Maybe the company you land a job at views work attire completely differently from the company in our scenario. In that case, please make sure that before starting your new job that you have a clear understanding of what is acceptable and what is not acceptable work attire and starting time. If the HR representative and/or hiring manager has not covered or answered one or more of your questions, make it a point to ask and receive an answer to alleviate any stress you may have about doing something that could be viewed negatively by your new colleagues and company as a new hire.

Some companies are even taking steps to combat some of the uncertainty by including frequently asked questions (FAQs) in their offer packet. Other organizations may share this pertinent information during orientation, which depending on the company, can occur anywhere from an hour to a couple of weeks after the start date where all new hires in a given time period (e.g. weekly, monthly) spend time together in a conference room learning about the organization, the different departments, key contacts across the organization, benefit enrollment (health insurance, 401(k) enrollment, etc.), and other important topics hand selected to give you a smooth start at their new company.

Next, we will review a series of key attributes that would be in your interest to understand and prepare for to ensure that you are properly maintaining your house/job. All of the following attributes I have experienced throughout my career.

One thing I found out early in my career was that whether I liked it or not, I would be asked on a daily basis to introduce myself on a teleconference/video conference or in person. Growing up I was an introvert, which the Oxford dictionary defines as "A person predominantly concerned with their own thoughts and feelings rather than with external things."[5] So how does this apply to what we are discussing? Although I tended to be more concerned about my own thoughts and feelings, the workforce was pushing me to grow more towards being an extrovert, which according to Oxford is "An outgoing, socially confident person."[6] Whether or not you are comfortable talking about your educational or professional experience to others, you will in most instances have to face and conquer that hurdle on a recurring basis.

Beginning during my college years, although I found myself relating more as an introvert, I took opportunities to lead class projects, which forced me to get comfortable standing in front of,

---

[5] https://en.oxforddictionaries.com/definition/introvert as recovered on December 2, 2016

[6] https://en.oxforddictionaries.com/definition/extrovert as recovered on December 2, 2016

speaking to, and conveying a message to an audience of business owners, professors, and classmates. I am a competitive individual that is always looking for an area to grow in. For me, this was a way to force myself out of my comfort zone and into a place of personal growth, which is uncomfortable at first. So, when it comes to your comfort level of introducing yourself to your colleagues, vendors, prospective vendors, or to a job candidate, the first thing you should ask yourself is do you relate more as an introvert or an extrovert? If you are naturally an extrovert, I would spend some time crafting and practicing an elevator message in front of a mirror or with a friend or family member.

An elevator message, also called an elevator pitch, is, in my opinion, a fifteen to thirty second introduction of yourself to a high-level employee of a company, such as a CEO. Why the short period of time? You may have ridden an elevator at one time or another in your life, such as at a hotel, a business, or an apartment complex. Some of you may have not been on an elevator, but if you were to ride one, there is a very short period of time from when you step on an elevator until you reach your intended floor and exit. If you step on an elevator that the CEO of your organization is on, in the short time before you or one of you reaches your intended floor, you would want to introduce yourself, briefly detailing what you do at their organization.

If you are an introvert, I recommend following the same steps as someone that is traditionally an extrovert, but rehearse with a friend or family member until you feel a hundred percent confident you can perform if given the opportunity. You may be wondering how likely it is that you will find yourself in an elevator with a key figure in your company. The probability of this occurring is higher if you work for a smaller company and lower if you find yourself working for a larger organization. So why do I bring this up if there is only a moderate likelihood of finding yourself on an elevator with a key figure from your company? One reason is that you want to be prepared in case that opportunity arises because first impressions mean a lot, and what bigger impression can be made other than having an opportunity to introduce yourself to a key figure in your company? The second reason is you will find yourself in the position of introducing yourself to others, albeit maybe not always to a key figure in your organization, on a daily basis. What the elevator pitch exercise does is prepare you for the most common situations as well as those less likely to arise.

Think about this for a minute. Let's say that you are an introvert that develops your elevator pitch. You have rehearsed until you are a hundred percent confident you can deliver it, and one day you step on the elevator as you do each work morning, and the CEO of your organization is already alone on the elevator car. He smiles, makes eye contact with you, and says, "Good morning. I am Tom, the CEO of your company. So, what do you do for us?" You respond with your carefully crafted elevator pitch, Tom smiles, shakes your hand, and thanks you for your service, telling you to keep up the good work for the company. How would that make you feel? It should make you feel awesome!

It makes no difference whether you are an introvert or extrovert. What matters most is that you put forth the required effort. If you are an extrovert and want to practice in front of an audience or an introvert that wants to practice and refine using a different method, there are many organizations out there that give you the opportunity to practice your speaking skills. The one organization that I am familiar with that fits into this boat is called Toastmasters. "Toastmasters International is a world leader in communication and leadership development. Our organization has more than 345,000 memberships. Members improve their speaking and leadership skills by attending one of the 15,900 clubs in 142 countries that make up our global network of meeting locations."[7] When building your elevator pitch, you should focus on three specific areas: 1) What department do you work in (marketing, finance, etc.)? 2) What do you do in your department at a high level?

---

7 http://www.toastmasters.org/About/Who-We-Are as recovered on December 2, 2016

3) Share the excitement and gratitude you have for the work you do and what your interests are. This may look something like, "Hi, my name is Justin Hayes. I work in accounting and finance. Currently, I execute the profit and loss statements for product line **X**. I would love to someday manage the team that executes the profit and loss statements for all of our product lines."

You should craft your individual elevator pitch in the manner you are comfortable speaking because you do not want to sound robotic while delivering your message. An easy rule of thumb that I have found to be helpful is that if you are unsure how to pronounce a word and/or its definition, do not use it because what would be more embarrassing than to be asked to explain right there on the spot? Also, you can elaborate further at your discretion, especially when you are introducing yourself in a teleconference or video conference or in person as it is common for individuals to have at least a minute or two to introduce themselves. The key here is to be comfortable and confident in yourself and your abilities because you are a smart, sharp individual who has a lot to offer a company, which is why a hiring manager should make the decision to hire you and not another job candidate!

Since these areas partially relate to a meeting setting, we will continue by reviewing meetings and proper meeting etiquette. A meeting setting can seem overwhelming for a new hire, and even a veteran, due to a variety of reasons. For one, you may be more of an introvert, and the thought of exhibiting extrovert qualities in a meeting room full of co-workers sends shivers down your back, especially those co-workers you have not met before. Two other reasons may be that the layout of the conference rooms does not follow logical order (e.g. alphabetical or numerical order) or that the meeting leader, the individual who has set up or called the meeting, did not circulate a meeting agenda prior to the meeting.

Let us now take a deeper dive into each of these scenarios. Try your best not to let being more of an introvert by nature interfere with a meeting. Sounds easy enough, but how exactly do you work through introvert qualities in a meeting? With any given meeting, you will either be a meeting leader or a participant that has been invited due to your expertise on one or more topics the meeting leader wishes to discuss. If either case arises, you will be prepared, and while you may be nervous about meeting participants you do not know, you should not be nervous about your areas of expertise because you already practiced and executed similar discussions in your interviews. While you may be a nervous wreck thinking about some meeting variables, you will not be nervous about your confidence because your education and/or previous work experience is fueling your participation in the discussion. You will not be asked to respond to or provide somebody else's viewpoint.

If you are the meeting leader, you should be the one who defines the subject, date/time, duration, location, participants, and the agenda of the meeting. When should you undertake the task to set up a meeting? There may be instances where your manager asks you to set up a meeting on a specific topic. If that happens, you should ask your manager what the meeting topic is and who should be invited. That is the easiest route for a meeting leader because someone else provides you all of the information required to set up a meeting. Another question you may also want answered is the timeframe your manager wants the meeting completed by. It is important to nail down the timing of the meeting because the deadline for the topic to be ironed out in the meeting may come and go before you are able to set up the meeting with the required participants. Although this is beyond your control, asking your manager ahead of time shows that you are being proactive instead of reactive, which is a preferred trait in the workforce regardless of field or industry.

The second route for you to be a meeting leader may come from encountering a daily task or project roadblock for which it is essential for you to uncover specific feedback from at least one other department to continue. In some cases, an email response may be sufficient to continue a daily task or project, but while an email may give you a specific answer or assumption, it usually does not explain how and why the specific answer or feedback came to be. This is important because there will be a point in time, possibly during a project checkpoint meeting with your superiors, where you will be asked why you chose a specific path. From my experience, you do not want to find yourself in a meeting with your superiors or colleagues being asked why you are proceeding in a given direction, and not have the why because your credibility will be in question as to whether you can complete further tasks and/ or projects in a full and comprehensive way.

There may be times where a question is far reaching, and it may be tough to recognize or speculate on an appropriate answer, but you want to try to limit those experiences as much as possible by staying on your areas of expertise. For instance, if you are in the marketing department and come to a point in your project where you need to project costs on a product for the next three years and you do not have that specific information to move forward, then here a business need has arisen for a meeting. In this example, you may want to list a member of the finance team as required in the meeting notice and denote other stakeholders in the project as optional so they are kept in the loop as to the progress of the task or project. This notice provides each stakeholder in the project a status on an area that needs addressing before moving forward. Also, there may be a stakeholder that already has some of the information you are looking for if they completed a similar project in the past, which may lower the likelihood you would need to hold a meeting in the first place. But the only way you will find this out is by including them on the meeting notice.

If the need remains, move forward with scheduling a meeting on the specific topic/s needed for you to continue your project. Then it is up to you as meeting leader to create a new meeting notice, including important information such as the meeting subject, date/time, duration, location, participants, and meeting agenda. The subject of the meeting, for example, could be something to the effect of "Project X Finance Touch Base." The meeting is not a check point; it is rather a touch base to discuss and solve a question or series of questions in order for you to continue your task. The body of the meeting notice is where you want to be sure to include an agenda, including each of the meeting participants and their expertise, or you can choose to include the meeting agenda in a separate attached document (Microsoft Word, PDF, etc.).

The time of a meeting should be chosen based on when you need the feedback to continue, the availability of your participants, and the availability of conference rooms in your location. There is an emphasis on increasing productivity and decreasing the amount of time in meetings, so try your best to limit the duration of the meeting. When you first enter the workforce, I recommend asking your manager or a colleague of yours how long a meeting on your chosen topic should last. Sometimes a meeting may be as short as fifteen minutes or as long as a whole day. It is up to you to use your best judgment along with the feedback from your manager and/or colleagues to define the duration of the meeting you are in charge of setting up.

The location of a meeting is dictated by how many individuals will be invited to attend. If two people in addition to the meeting leader (in this case you) will be participating then you will only need a conference room with three seats, not a larger conference room that holds twenty. Your manager, colleagues and/or HR representative will be able to help you learn how many conference rooms are in your building, their locations, and what the range of attendees is for each. For example, at some organizations, you are able to view the number of attendees that will fit in each conference room when booking (e.g. Conference Room A; 1 – 5 seats).

As the meeting leader, the final key topic to tackle is the meeting agenda. The meeting agenda should be either included in the body of the meeting notice or attached to the meeting notice in Microsoft Word/PDF form. Meeting agenda elements to be included are: subject, date/time, duration, location, participants, and the topic(s) that will be discussed and completed. In today's fast-paced business world, the meeting agenda is becoming an old art form, meaning that meeting agendas are not used correctly or even at all, which leads to more meetings and lower meeting satisfaction for employees at those companies. But for the sake of meeting efficiency, which includes leaving the meeting having completed all meeting agenda items and respecting all meeting participant's time, having and following a meeting agenda is the number one way to increase meeting efficiency.

Another recommendation to increase the focus on the meeting and the meeting agenda is to include the names of the departments and respective individuals that will be responsible for solving or helping to solve each agenda item next to each agenda item. For instance, if the agenda item is "Projecting Future Product Cost," an appropriate notation would be "Projecting Future Product Cost – Finance: Justin Hayes." If you are unsure which individual or department will be able to cover the meeting topic, it is okay to write "All" next to that particular agenda item or a specific department, such as "Finance."

You not only need an emphasis on creating and including the meeting agenda within the meeting notice, but as meeting leader, it is critical that you follow the meeting agenda once the meeting begins. The last thing you want to do is not follow the meeting agenda and have the meeting time run out without completing each meeting agenda item. This would mean wasted time for everyone involved because you most likely will have to schedule a follow-up meeting to finish discussing the items on the agenda.

An easy way to think about this is research and execution. The research part comes when you are setting up the meeting, and the execution piece is ensuring that you do not leave the meeting without each meeting agenda item being completed or, at the very least, addressed along with identifying those individuals responsible for following up. Not only will you feel good about the meeting because you were able to obtain the information to continue your project, but the meeting attendees will thank you for valuing their time and staying on topic.

Now, there are the customary greetings of "Hi, how are you today? How was your weekend?", but those pleasantries do not need to take up fifteen minutes of a thirty-minute meeting. I have witnessed this too many times to count where only fifteen minutes are left in a meeting, and the meeting leader has not even started the items on the meeting agenda. I have also witnessed too many meeting leaders not including a meeting agenda in the meeting notice. Some people think that the subject is all that is important, but if you are a meeting leader, take it upon yourself to set an example for yourself, your department, and your organization.

The second way you can find yourself included in a meeting is as a participant. The meeting subject, date/time, duration, location, participants, and the agenda have already been identified and sent out electronically by the meeting leader. It is imperative for the meeting leader to include an agenda in the meeting notice because, as a participant, you otherwise may have no clue as to why you are being invited to this meeting. If you are invited to a meeting and there is no meeting agenda on the meeting notice, do not hesitate to initiate a call or email with the meeting leader to ask specifically why you need to attend. If the meeting leader still does not include an agenda with their meeting notice with that information, make sure at the very least you know why your meeting attendance is being requested, so you can document exactly why you are attending and what expertise you are being expected to provide at the meeting. You want to show the meeting leader and other meeting participants that you are well prepared. I have witnessed meetings where all meeting participants prepared and others where one or several meeting participants were not prepared. Whether you think so or not, people notice.

Up until the meeting, it is your responsibility to know exactly what the expectations of your meeting attendance are because once the meeting starts all participants are under the impression that everyone is fully prepared. I have been on both sides of the coin at different points in my career. Take my word, and do your best to make sure you are prepared for all meetings you are requested to attend, because if you thought being nervous and embarrassed during a job interview was tough to handle, imagine being in a meeting with your manager and colleagues and asked to answer a question well within your area of expertise and not providing an adequate response due to lack of preparation. Preparing for meetings is well within your control, so always be ready for meetings you are asked to attend.

Regardless of whether you are the meeting leader or a participant, the actions you take in a meeting are the same. In a meeting where you are not familiar with the participants, I suggest that if seated, stand up and introduce yourself and shake the other participants' hands. You do not need to do this in successive meetings with the same individuals, but I do suggest this approach in the first meeting with individuals you have not yet met. This is not mandatory to follow, but is regarded to be respectful and professional.

Also, some of you will be in positions that conduct business with outside vendors. An outside vendor is an outside company that does or wishes to do business with your company. In a meeting that includes outside vendors, which you presumably have not met previously, you should not only stand up, introduce yourself, and shake their hands, but also exchange business cards in a similar way to in-person interviews. Business cards should be exchanged so that all individuals have the current contact information for each meeting participant, which makes it easier for after-meeting follow-up.

The company name, employee name, title, physical mailing address, email address, and fax number are some of the most common information included on a business card. You have learned how important it is to exchange business cards in an in-person interview and meeting setting, but how do you actually go about ordering your own business cards? Ordering your business cards is something that may be covered during your new hire orientation or a topic that you can ask your manager about.

Depending on the company you work for, you may be able to expect to receive your business cards in a couple of weeks to a month or more. The timing is based on the frequency and quantity your company orders business cards in. If you are invited to a meeting before your business cards have arrived, do not panic; merely communicate to meeting attendees that you are new to the company and have not yet received your business cards. Business cards do not necessarily need to be exchanged with individuals within the same organization, but it is a nice gesture, especially when you first meet in person.

When my first business cards were delivered once I was out of college, I remember thinking to myself that I wanted to give all my friends and family one to show that all of the time and energy I exhausted in college was starting to pay off. You may have a similar feeling when you are handed your first business card! Some technology-driven organizations are moving away from business cards and are using social media, such as LinkedIn in its place. If you encounter this in the workplace, I would be sure to ask which social media platform(s) the individuals and their respective companies use, and connect with them on those platforms.

Whether you work at a small or large organization, the logic to the conference room floor layout can be confusing unless you designed it yourself. If you look at a floor layout from left to right like a rectangle (with the long side of the rectangle at the base), the mind of an individual tends logically to believe that the conference room floor layout progression should be 1-2-3-4, A-B-C-D or a combination such as 1A, 1B, 1C, 1D. Sometimes the layout of conference rooms follows this progression and sometimes it does not follow any rational progression.

Why is this important? What if on your first day you have a meeting scheduled in 1A at 9:00 am? The building your employer is located in only has one floor, so you do not need to take multiple floors into account. At 8:55 am, you begin to walk to your meeting at the end of the building that would, in theory, house the conference rooms with the number 1 and letter A. You arrive to the area in the building you logically concluded that the conference room should be at 8:59 am only to find that the conference room nearest you is actually 1C. So, now you start frantically searching around the first floor for conference room 1A, and you finally end up locating conference room 1A in the middle of the first floor, not at either end, let alone the logical end of the building. By now it is 9:03 am, and you enter the meeting late on your first day with all of the other meeting participants noticing your late arrival.

I give this extreme example because it could happen to anyone, and it is my job to prepare you for such a situation so that you do your due diligence to prepare and understand where each of the conference rooms are located in your building, even if their layout makes little or no sense at all. How should you conduct your research and due diligence on conference room floor layouts? Search your company intranet for a layout of the building with each of the conference rooms clearly labeled. Often the conference room floor layout is in Microsoft Word or PDF document form. Next, print this document out for the times you are requested to lead and/or participate in a meeting being held in a conference room. Sometimes your office floor layout and arrangement may put you near other meeting attendees, so another action you can take is to walk together with another meeting attendee to the meeting. This way you will be covered by paper and by brain power!

Dinner etiquette can seem overwhelming if you have never had an experience to fall back on for reference. The context of dinner etiquette that I am referring to occurs after you have been hired at a company, not interview dinner etiquette, although many of my recommendations are easily adaptable between the two scenarios.

An invitation to attend a business dinner can come from any number of sources. Some of the more common sources are your manager, one of your colleagues, administrative assistant, administrative assistant at a vendor/supplier company, counterpart at a vendor/supplier company, or a representative from a conference/summit you may be attending. The information that is generally included in a dinner invitation is the invitees, the restaurant name and address, reservation time, and associated time zone. The time zone is important because if you are located in the Eastern Time Zone, your vendor/supplier organization is in the Central Time Zone and the dinner invitation is at a conference/summit you both are attending is in the Pacific Time Zone, a lot of confusion could ensue. I have had experiences where this exact scenario has played out, making this point vitally important for you to consider, especially if you have been charged with setting up the meeting.

Let's assume you are not the individual scheduling and sending out the dinner invitations, but rather are on the receiving end of a business dinner invitation. After you receive the dinner invitation, it is important to identify what the required dress will be for the dinner. The dress attire for a business dinner will be dictated by the restaurant selection. For example, a fine dining restaurant will require business professional to formal and so forth. This is not always the case, however, so it is vital for you to reach out to the dinner organizer and/or your colleagues attending the dinner to gain a clear understanding of what the expected dress will be. Showing up to the dinner in appropriate attire is a great first step, whether you are a new hire or a seasoned veteran. Always remember that just as it is important to wear proper the attire to a job interview, the same goes for a business dinner.

A business dinner should not be treated like you and your friends are going to the bar. Rather, a business dinner is directly tied to your livelihood. Making the mistake of treating the business dinner any differently could turn it from a blessing to a curse in an instant. The next area to focus on with the business dinner is what to order from the menu. It has been my experience that the dinner organizer/company representative will be the first to order, and so it is important to gain a sense of what the organizer is ordering. For example, if the dinner organizer orders the most inexpensive entrée on the menu, it would not be wise for you to go ahead and order the most expensive entrée. If appetizers are ordered, the dinner organizer will be the one to order them. Remember, this is a business dinner, not a personal dinner.

My experience in this capacity has also been that the dinner organizer will gain a consensus from the dinner attendees before ordering any such appetizers. I have been invited to a number of business dinners over my professional career, and there have been instances where appetizers were ordered for the table and others where appetizers were not ordered, so it is not a forgone conclusion that appetizers will be ordered for the table. If you always order appetizers when you are out to eat and encounter a business dinner where appetizers are not ordered, do not comment to anyone at the dinner that someone is being cheap by not ordering them. Employees who make comments along those lines are often not invited to additional dinners while with the company.

To be crystal clear here, the one rule I always follow in a business dinner setting is that I never order an entrée more expensive than the dinner organizer and/or the highest- ranking individual (manager, director, vice president, etc.) at my company, both when the dinner organizer is and is not from my company. Why? Because while you may not conduct future business with the other company at dinner, you will be seeing and working with those individuals from your company. It is not worth ordering the most expensive entrée on the menu just because you will not have to pay for it out of your personal monies or because your friends always do when they attend a business dinner.

I had an experience where, as a manager, one of my direct reports decided that, because the employee was at a business dinner and would not be held financially responsible for the cost of the dinner, the employee could order anything off of the menu. What this goes back to is quality decision making. Is this the type of individual that you want on your company work team, one that maxes out the amount his company or partner company has to pay for dinner? Can this individual be trusted with balancing a budget or completing assignments and projects accurately and on-time? Trust me that you do not want your manager or someone else in management to start questioning your integrity as an employee. It goes without saying that this employee of mine never attended another business dinner I was responsible for and caused me to question his integrity. For this reason, I follow the aforementioned advice regarding business dinners and suggest that you do too so you do not end up jeopardizing your job and livelihood!

We have already covered the importance of networking through vehicles such as LinkedIn. Networking can also take another route that can either be formal or informal. This route is referred to as mentorship. Mentorship, as defined by the Oxford dictionary, is "The guidance provided by a mentor, especially an experienced person in a company or educational institution."[8] Mentorship is a great way for you to network within your company with an

8 https://en.oxforddictionaries.com/definition/mentorship as recovered on January 13, 2017

employee who has experience and longevity. I recommend identifying a couple of potential mentors at your organization who are at least one level higher than you and located in another department. For instance, if you are a tax analyst, you would want to identify potential mentors outside of the accounting department who are at least a senior tax analyst or higher. It is important to follow these two criteria since one of the main benefits of a mentorship relationship is to learn about other departments and their function within the organization because you will have an interest to advance your career at some point, and what better way to help you identify whether or not that particular area could be a potential fit for you than to network with someone that is living and breathing that type of work on a daily basis?

Selecting a mentor who is at least one level higher than you will give you the ability to learn what it takes to advance in the company from someone who has already lived it. You may learn from your mentor that your company is big on training or employees who look to further their education (e.g. valuing a master's degree over a bachelor's degree). While most companies will have a mission statement and values, seldom do they cover this level of detail. One of the best ways to gain this level of detail is to network within your organization and learn from those individuals through a mentorship relationship. Lastly, by taking advantage of a mentorship opportunity, you may find yourself interested in the department of your mentor, when you may not have otherwise discovered your interest in that department. If down the road, you choose to apply for an opening in your mentor's department your mentor would become that much more of an asset for you. For example, what could be better than having your mentor write a recommendation for you to join their department?

I recommend that you find, start, and maintain a mentor relationship with at least one individual from your company. This is what I refer to as an internal mentor because the mentor is working at your company. Each company has a different philosophy at a top level. Some companies have a formal mentorship program where you are required to complete assignments at different points of the mentorship, while others may have a less formalized approach. You will want to touch base with your HR representative and/or your manager for more information on if they offer a mentorship program and if so what the requirements to join are.

I also recommend that you find, start, and maintain a mentor relationship with at least one individual outside of your company, what I refer to as an external mentor. Why is it important to have both an internal and external mentor? As life events, such as marriage and the birth of children occur, they may lead to a potential shift in your interests. You may be faced with making decisions that may take you away from your current company. For example, if you get engaged and your fiancé lands a great job that doubles his pay and/or increases responsibilities in a different city or state than you currently work in, you may now be in search of a job closer to where your fiancés' new job will be geographically located. If your company has a presence in that new city or state, you could explore open opportunities to see if there is a match. If not, you will be taking your job search externally (i.e. outside of your current company), and this would be a topic that you would not want to share with an internal mentor. You could, however, share this information with an external mentor.

Who would qualify as an external mentor for you? An external mentor may be a former coach, a teacher, or other individual who does not work at your current company who you respect and would value honest feedback from. Again, this is your decision, and as such you will be the one to evaluate whether or not your external mentor will meet your needs.

It is important to show up to all of your mentorship meetings with an agenda, the same as when you are a meeting leader. As the mentee, it is a hundred percent up to you, not the mentor, to create the agenda. If you show up to a mentorship meeting without an agenda, then the meeting becomes a general conversation about topics unrelated to your work, your organization, or your career goals, which is not the goal of mentorship. Another one of the benefits of creating and following an agenda is that you will be able to check off all of the agenda items once they are covered, creating a sense of accomplishment in maximizing the mentor-mentee relationship. Mentorship relationships have been valuable to me and will continue to be a part of my professional growth and development and so too should it be for you.

The topic we are going to conclude with pertains to aggregating all of your accomplishments into one easy-to-find and update document for performance review assessments and resume building. I like to call this aggregation a "Brag sheet" because it is truly a reflection of what you have completed and is a form of bragging. The importance of a Brag sheet is twofold: performance reviews and resume building. Unless you own your own company, you will most likely be subjected to a form of performance review at your company.

At a summary level, a performance review is how you performed against your goals for a given time period (e.g. ninety days, six months, annually). You should be able to see how a Brag sheet can be helpful here because as you complete daily tasks and projects throughout the year you can quickly jump over to your aggregated document and extract that important information, such as each daily task or project completed, the duration, the individuals or departments included, and a takeaway such as, "Analysis was completed that revealed our pricing was much higher than our top competitors, so I worked with X individual in Y department on our pricing including lowering our input costs so we could be more competitive; new pricing implemented on mm/dd/yyyy."

You may think that you will remember each and every detail of each project you complete, but we are all human, and the best method I have found to ensure I remember successful tasks when performance review time rolls around is to have an electronic file that I can quickly refer back to. This exact method has been helpful to me after finding that even I was prone to forgetting every detail over the course of a year. The Brag sheet is something that is easy to do and within your control, so it is a no brainer for me and should be for you too!

The second way you can maximize your Brag sheet is for building and updating your resume. Whether you utilize the career services department at your college or request help from an expert in resume building and writing, they will all ask you to identify and explain your accomplishments and areas of expertise with examples to support each in order to build or update your resume. Instead of having to carve time out of one or several evenings trying to remember and document all of this information, wouldn't it be nice to turn your computer on and open up a file and print? You can save yourself a lot of time and energy if you follow my recommendation and created and maintained your very own Brag sheet.

To help prepare for your first or next performance review, please practice by filling out the Performance Review Preparation Worksheet.

PERFORMANCE REVIEWS PREPARATION WORKSHEET

Directions: **Answer the following statements and questions to the best of your ability.**

Name 3-5 of your top projects / assignments / high-profile requests (Director Level or above) from the previous time period (i.e. last 3/6/9/12 months depending on your Companyâ€™s Performance Review cycle) the different areas or departments (i.e. Accounting/ Legal/Marketing/etc.) you worked with, the main task or ask (i.e. profitability/new product development research/etc.) for each, the time spent on each top project/assignment/high-profile request, what your contributions were for each, what the out outcome was of each and how the tasks or asks were tied to the mission/goals of the Company.

What job training have you completed over the prior period? This can include both company sponsored and/or job training that was administered by a 3rd party (i.e. American Marketing Association Market Research Boot camp). The job training can be training completed on-site, off-site and/or online.

Conversely, what training do you wish to complete over the next time period that will help you do your job more proficiently and/or is a stepping stone in your future career plans with the

Company? Company's most likely will not support or sponsor (i.e. pay for and allow you to be away from work without using Paid Time Off or Vacation time) training that is not directly tied to your current job or a job interest at your current company. This practice is implemented in order to deter current employees to use a Company to pay for and allow time away off from work, only to leave the Company and receive a benefit (higher starting base salary, job title, etc.) from the training from a previous employer.

What other areas or interests do you have with your current Company in which you may want the opportunity to shadow and/or learn more about during the upcoming time period?

What 3 areas do you feel are you strengths' that may be able to help other areas or departments at your Company? Maybe you can offer to hold a lunch & learn where you can teach another area or department about your strengths and how they benefit the Company. Managers love to see employees that are engaged, proactive and willing to help others:

What 3 areas would you like to improve on during the next time period? Everyone has things that they can improve on. I know I do. This is the time to swallow your pride and continue to grow as an employee and as an individual.

The best way I have learned and gained experience over the years is with and through hands on practicing. And I have included the following 5 Case Challenges for that very reason; To give you another way or method to read, review and answer the associated questions with building your house.

CASE CHALLENGES

Case #1

<u>Company Decision</u>

Company 'House Time' is a diversified family run Company, meaning they offer products that serve different market segments. The products House Time manufacturer and sell are in the child safety industry. From gates that separate an upper level hallway to where steps that connect that floor to the lower floor, or from the first floor to the basement, to baby video monitors that give parents of a newborn or a toddler the bird's eye view of their child's crib from anywhere in the house to a video receiver that can be viewed by parents anywhere in the house. And for those parents who have a babysitter or a nanny that take care of that newborn or toddler, the parents can even have the video feed projected out to their smart phones with an application. House Time are the market leaders with over 75% of the products they manufacturer and sell to consumers. Their competition is constantly thinking and researching new product concepts above and beyond their own product offerings with the hope of gaining market share back from House Time in the high risk, high reward industry of child safety.

A new startup Company in the child safety industry named 'Jump' has reached out to the CEO of House Time because Jump had been contacted by show producers for the hit TV show Park Tank, and subsequently taped a segment to be nationally televised in an upcoming episode on the JBC network. In the segment, Jumps' Vice President of New Business Development pitches their new product to the 5 Park Tank investors, hoping for a business deal that would bring one or several of the investors onboard to fully or partially financially fund this proposed new product. Jump was also interested in the Park Tank opportunity because whether a business deal was struck, the segment would be watched by millions of American households, some who might be so intrigued in the new product that they may want to purchase anyways, even if one or several of the well-known investors did not end up backing it.

Fast forward; the taping of Jump's segment has concluded on the Los Angeles set of Park Tank. The contact that Jump made was in good faith to confirm JBC will indeed be airing the segment with Jump on an upcoming episode. The schedule had even been set so Jump knew the exact date and time the segment would be airing. Furthermore, the details of the contact between Jump and House Time included the topic of since Jumps' new product is complimentary to another child safety product that is not currently in their portfolio, but is in House Times' portfolio, Jump needed a partner, an exclusive partner that would be willing to co-market Jumps new product. So, it is with this in mind that Jump's CEO reaches out to Jimmy James, the CEO of House Time to garner their interest to partner with Jump as an exclusive partner for their new product. Because JBC demands all companies who go on Park Tank to sign Non-Disclosure Agreements and all put under a gag order, Jump cannot share the details and result of their pitch to the Park Tank investors (i.e. whether Jump got a deal or not, and if Jump got a deal, what the terms were and which investor/s made it.) until the TV segment had aired. So, House Time would not know the result of the segment until everyone else in America that watched also learned the result, whether positive or negative, whether Jump got a deal or Jump did not land a deal.

However, all signs from Jump to Jimmy James at House Time point to a positive outcome on Park Tank, but Jimmy has no guaranteed assurance on the episode one way or another. At this point, flipping a coin would provide about as much in way as a prediction as Jump is providing House Time. Jimmy is still pondering the partnership with his lead counsel (attorney) the week of the scheduled episode airing when Jump calls asking once again about the proposed partnership. Still perplexed and unsure of the right avenue because not only does Jimmy not know the outcome of the Park Tank segment, but he also doesn't know how Jump's product was portrayed during the segment. If Jump's product and presentation was shown as part of a comedic segment, it would make total sense for Jimmy and House Time to pull the plug on any potential deal. As sometimes with media and TV specifically, a Company and/or product may not be shown in the greatest light, such as most reality TV shows. TV producers know that certain segments of their viewing audience love drama, even if it comes at someone or something's expense. With this being crunch time, Jimmy is weighing both of those pieces when Jump adds even more confusion and complexity to the equation. Jump wants House Time to purchase 1,000 of their new to the world child safety product with no past or current sales before the airing of the upcoming Park Tank episode, with half of the money to be paid to Jump up front (i.e. the date in which the contract is agreed upon and signed by both parties) and the second half of the money payable in 30 days. With a per unit cost to House Time of $100 means House Time would be on the hook for $50,000 now and $50,000 in 30 days.

It is now Friday evening of the weekend Park Tank is going to air with Jump's pitch to its investors when Jump's CEO asks Jimmy one last time if House Time will strike a deal with Jump prior to knowing the outcome, how the product (which needs House Time's product to maximize its accuracy and effectiveness) is portrayed to the Park Tank investors and TV audience and secondly fronting $50,000 for the 1,000 units without any prior sales history.

Answer the Following Questions About the Case:

1. Should Jimmy and House Time make the pre-show deal? Why or why not?
2. What additional information, if provided, would strengthen your confidence level in your answer in question #1?
3. Do you think Jump's CEO is acting in an ethical manner by first asking House Time about his thoughts on a partnership and then in a high-stake pressure cooker in the days leading up to the episode airing, without sharing the result of their segment?
4. If Jimmy makes the deal & Jump does not receive an offer and subsequent deal from a Park Tank investor/s, House Time would be out $50,000 the day Jump and House Time strike a deal and the second $50,000 30-days from the deal struck date. And as after the show airs, no consumers purchase Jump's and House Time's co-marketed product combo. Because of this decision Jimmy and House Time have no other option, but to lay off 2 employees to offset the $100,000 cost of his decision. Does this extra information alter in one way or another your initial answer in question #1?
5. What processes or safeguards would you put in place if you were the CEO of House Time, Jimmy James, to help guide future decision making in similar business situations?

Case #2

Interviewee Dilemma

You are a month away from Graduation when you get a phone call from an HR representative from a Company whose open position you had applied to three weeks ago. On the second ring, you pick up and the individual on the other side of the line starts the conversation by identifying themselves as Sarah, an HR representative from Company X. Sarah asks how you are doing.

You respond, "Great, how are you?" Sarah proceeds to tell you she is calling in regards to a position you had applied to and that upon review of the initial list of job applicants, the hiring manager has an interest in you coming to the Company X Global Headquarters for an in-person interview. After negotiating a date and time that is available for you and the interview team, you thank the HR Rep Sarah for her time and close the conversation by communicating your continued interest in the position and how excited you are to meet her and the interview team in person. After hanging up the phone you are feeling great, so you share the fresh news with your roommate, who is also your best friend and #1 supporter behind your parents.

The two weeks between learning of the interview and the actual interview date goes by lightning fast. During that timeframe you complete additional research about Company X, including the history, main products and distribution channels along with the brick & mortar and e-tailer's where their products are sold. Even learning the price points of Company X's products taught you whether they sell luxury or affordable products. The scheduled interview date and time approaches and you are confident that you will knock it out of the park. You arrive a few minutes early to calm yourself, gain your composure, take a couple deep breaths and clear your mind of distractions. You exit your car and lock up and as you are walking towards the entrance to the Company's headquarters, you are in a positive mood and just know you will end up being offered the position once the entire hiring process has played itself out. When you open the front door and take your initial steps into the Company lobby, your attention can't help but notice the décor on the walls and built into some of the furniture pieces. The walls are covered with the taxidermized heads of over a dozen wild & exotic animals and the two glass end tables on either side of the couch with what appeared to be taxidermized feet of elephants. You are immediately taken back by such a sight, especially in the lobby of a pet safety product Company. You continue the process by checking in with the receptionist and are told the HR Rep you had spoken with will be right down to greet you and begin the in-person interview process. As envisioned for several days in your mind, the entire onsite interview process goes by without a hitch or even an unsure question and response, you thank the interview team for their time and collect each of their business' cards. You now leave the Company HQ and proceed to walk out to your car with mixed emotions. Yes, on the business side of things the interview transpired just as you pictured it would, however you still cannot wrap your head around the sight you viewed inside the lobby. And with you being one of those right brained human beings that processes and remembers information best through pictures and everything in the visual portfolio, it is hard to forget. Once you arrive home, you still do the right thing and hand write a thank you note to each of the employees you interviewed with on the interview team. Once the thank you notes are on their way in the mail via the United States Postal Service, you continue networking, searching and applying to the jobs that align with your entry lever career education, skills and internship experience. A week goes by without any communication from the company you had interviewed with just 7 days ago. Relieved to an extent that you do not need to wrestle with the idea of making a difficult decision as to whether to negotiate and/or accept an offer from, in your eyes an unethical company, but also wanting the job and feeling as though you had aced the interview. You have very much mixed emotions, when a day late as you are continuing the job search process, your cell phone rings with a recently familiar number that can only be the company calling to communicate a verbal offer or that another candidate was selected for the position. You experience butterflies as you sigh, take a deep breath and answer. What occurs next is the HR representative shares with you that the company had just finished all interviews and debriefs with all of the interviewers and reached the consensus that you are the best candidate for the job and so they wanted to make you a verbal offer. A wave of happiness comes over you, but still in the back of your mind lies the scenes you saw at the company's headquarters.

Since you read The House of You: 5 Workforce Preparation Tips For a Successful Career, you have already completed your Job Offer Decision Guiding Worksheet, which covers all of the key areas of a job offer, what is acceptable and how important each is to you: The base salary, variable pay (bonus performance pay), health insurance, whether or not a 401 (k) plan and a 401 (k) plan company match (i.e. the company will match a percentage of your elected contributions, such as matching the first 3% you contribute at 100%, which equates to a total 401 (k) contribution of 6%). The last factor in which to consider is whether relocation assistance is being offered to you. Since the company headquarters is located only 20 minutes from your house, the company will not be offering relocation assistance for this position.

You thank the HR representative for their time and ask if it is ok to inform him/her of your decision within 48 hours. Sarah confirms that 48 hours is ok with her and the company and so you hang up the phone and again, your stomach starts to churn. What a dilemma...

Flash Questions about Interviewing related to the Case:

1. What 2 steps should you take with your social media accounts prior to applying for an internship or a full-time position?

   (Make accounts that can be private and or take down or untag yourself in phots that may negatively impact whether you get considered for an interview or receive a job/internship offer.)

2. What 4 things should you take to every in-person interview?

   1. Enough copies of your resume on resume paper, 2. A portfolio with work/school project samples, 3. Business cards and 4. A portfolio (can be the same portfolio as #2 that has a notepad included) that you can use to take notes and refer to when asking interviewers questions about their background, the position and the company.

Answer the Following Questions About the Case:

1. Complete you Job Offer Decision Guiding Worksheet in a matrix form, with a column for each Job Offer element, your ranking with 1 being the most important, and another column for what you would accept in an offer for each of the Job Offer elements.

2. What ethical concern/s could you or other potential job candidates have with the Company in the case?

3. Do you or would you share your ethical concerns with other potential job candidates on social media or a website like the GlassDoor.com?

4. What moral obligation if any would you have if this case was about you as the interviewee?

5. Who would you reach out to in your network, if anyone for advice, to help you in the decision-making process and why?

6. If you were the interviewee in the case, would you accept the job offer? Why, or why not?

Case #3

5 Years In: How is your Financial Health?

Exactly 6 years ago today (5 full work years) you began your professional career working as a Staff Accountant at a Fortune 100 Company, and one of the Top Companies in the state of Florida. Let us refer to this company as Company D for the sake of this case study. One of the distinguishing characteristics of the offer you received from Company D 5 years ago was their benefit plan, a benefit plan that was different from all of the companies you had worked for before and earned offers from when you started researching & applying to jobs that your professional experience and education was a fit for outside of the company you were working for at that time. Additionally, not only was an appealing year around climate with close beaches important in your opinion especially since you were single, but so was a competitive base salary and variable bonus performance pay that was based off both your personal performance (otherwise called the performance review) and the Company's performance (i.e. did the company make money or lose money?).

Although listed at the bottom of your offer letter from Company D, but most important to you was the benefits package, which included medical, dental & vision insurance, 401(k) (pretax and post-tax Roth) options and the stipend of vacation or paid time off (PTO). You are still single as we sit today and so you wanted to take stock of where you are from a high-level financial perspective, both the inflow (income) and outflow (expenses) pertinent to your job. So, what we are going to look at next are each of the first 5 years of income and expenses related to your job, split out by calendar year (January-December) which also coincides with Company Dâ€™s fiscal year. After all information is presented there will be follow-up questions. This is extremely important for you to first of all understand what is generally included in a job offer, but also to help you picture where you may be at financially after 5 years of work.

Income/Expense/Retirement	All Benefits	Year 1	Year 2	Year 3	Year 4	Year 5
Income	Base Salary (Gross)	$50,000	$52,000	$57,000	$59,000	$61,000
Income	Variable Bonus Performance Pay	10%	10%	10%	15%	15%
Expense	Medical Insurance	$1,200	$1,300	$1,400	$1,600	$1,800
Expense	Vision Insurance	$100	$115	$130	$140	$150
Expense	Dental Insurance	$240	$250	$260	$270	$280
Retirement	401(k) Plan Employee Contribution	$5,000	$5,200	$5,700	$5,900	$6,100
Retirement	401(k) Plan Company Match	$5,000	$5,200	$5,700	$5,900	$6,100

* Note that we will not take into account taxes, since taxes vary by state, and locale and are often updated from year to year.

Answer the Following Questions About the Case:

1. Assume that you received your full Variable Bonus Performance Pay for Year 1, Year 2, Year 3, and 50% of your Variable Bonus Performance Pay for Year 4 and Year 5, what would your Total Variable Bonus Performance Pay be for Year 1, Year 2, Year 3, Year 4 and Year 5?Please explain your answer.

    a. Using your answer to the above, what would be your Total Income for Year 1, Year 2, Year 3, Year 4 and Year 5? Please explain your answer.

2. If you received your full Variable Bonus Performance Pay for all 5 years, what would your Total Income be for Year 1, Year 2, Year 3, Year 4 and Year 5? Please explain your answer.

3. Using the information in the above table with no changes, what are your Total Expenses for Year 1, Year 2, Year 3, Year 4 and Year 5?

4. If your Variable Bonus Performance Pay was eliminated in Year 4, with everything else staying the same as the above table, what would be the Total of Income and Expenses? Please explain your answer.

5. If you had a goal to amass $200,000 in your first 5 years working (after expenses, but including your Employee Contributions and Company Match, with both contributions of a growth rate of 12% in each of the 5 years), did you hit your goal? Why or why not? Please explain your answers.

6. What would your Total Expenses be in each of the 5 years, if you eliminated Vision Insurance in Year 3, Year 4 and Year 5?

7. Assuming there are no changes in the above table, and both the Employee Contribution and the Company Match each earned 5% in Year 1, Year 2 and Year 3, while earning 8%

in Year 4 and Year 5, what would be the Total of Income, Expenses and Retirement be for Year 1, Year 2, Year 3, Year 4 and Year 5? Please explain your answer.

Case #4

Should Employee Start to Look for Job Outside Current Company?

Jerry is a loyal employee who has worked diligently and faithfully for the past 10 years at the same company. He even was awarded as one of the few employees with the most years of service at a quarterly Companywide meeting last week. Graduating college with a Bachelor's degree in Management, Jerry was riding a high wave with lofty expectations to be in a Senior Management role after 5 years if he caught on with the right Company that was in search of a high octane 21-year-old who prided himself on leading team projects and excelling in individual projects, especially when the project included an accompanying oral presentation.

Jerry was a natural extrovert that always felt like he was teaching his spectators about a new and exciting subject, which made Jerry at ease standing & speaking in front of groups of Professor's along with his student peers. The right Company did indeed come calling at just shy of 3 months past his spring graduation. The Company was intrigued with Jerry's fire to complete his projects, even in the eyes of adversity, and the fact that he had a portfolio with him at his interviews to highlight his key accomplishments and give his on-site interviewer's samples of his transferrable work from college to the workforce. Jerry's portfolio supplemented his excellent visual, verbal & non-verbal communication when Jerry responded to the questions being asked of him.

Fast forward to 3 years, Jerry was offered the position he interviewed for and through the end of the interview process, Jerry had been promised a promotion by his hiring Manager if he went back to school and earned an MBA (Masters of Business Administration). Fueled again by a challenge and a goal of this proposal, goal and achievement-oriented Jerry made the decision to move forward, study and take the GMAT exam, especially since the Company covered the cost of the exam. The GMAT exam is an entrance exam most students have to take in order to be accepted into a Graduate program at a college or university. Jerry did phenomenal on the GMAT and was afforded the opportunity to choose the school he wanted to attend for his MBA, which was something Jerry did not take for granted because some of Jerry's friends either did not score high enough on the GMAT to have the luxury of choosing or did not score high enough to be accepted into any MBA program.

Since Jerry's Company's' headquarters resided near a local University that he could enroll in and take evening classes once or twice a week after the end of his full-time workday (most days were 8am-5pm), the local university was the logical choice to attend. Once enrolled, Jerry was once again on his way to accomplish big goals. Although it took Jerry a couple of his first MBA class sessions to get back into the swing of sitting through long lectures, working on class projects both individually and on teams with students with similar and diverse backgrounds and skill-sets. Even if there was a period of time for transition back into school learning, Jerry enjoyed the complete learning experience because it offered him an opportunity to expand on his breadth and depth of knowledge in subjects, he was familiar with and to start building a base of knowledge in those subjects he was less familiar with. For Jerry, Undergrad was an outlet to mostly learn theories & definitions of key terms and processes, while the MBA program challenged him to also apply those theories, key terms & processes, which were supplemented by each students' professional experience in their careers thus far.

Jerry excelled in each of his classes and ended up graduating and earning his MBA degree a mere 2 years after starting, which was a colossal accomplishment that no one in his immediate or extended family had yet conquered. Jerry would undoubtedly be rewarded with the promised promotion after completion of the MBA program. Or would he? As the time for Jerry's first performance review since earning his MBA was approaching, Jerry could only think that the upcoming promotion would be the big break of his career and part of his goal to attaining a Senior Management position after 5 years at his Company. The promised promotion would also afford him a vehicle to give him and his family some much needed financial security he and his family had never seen. The time for Jerry's performance review came and went and in a surprising and stunning turn of events, Jerry was in the end not offered the promotion that was promised to him. Among other feelings Jerry was feeling, Jerry felt let down and taken advantage of. The Company besides pulling a fast one on Jerry about the promised promotion, also had Jerry in a contractual obligation in which he had to stay at the current Company for a time frame of 2 years, or else he was on the hook for the full cost of the tuition & books the Company paid on Jerry's behalf throughout the entirety of his MBA coursework. This type of contractual obligation is commonplace at Company's and is a form of insurance taken out so that the employee whose education was almost entirely paid for by the Company, would not earn the degree and bolt for another Company at the first instant after graduation. So if Jerry wanted to leave the company before the 2 year clock was up, he would be expected to pay the Company back the approximate amount of $30,000 it had paid for the duration of Jerry's MBA program before leaving for a new job and new Company. What an unfortunate situation Jerry is now in.

Answer the Following Questions About the Case:

1. Should Jerry be looking for a new job outside of his current Company? Why or why not?

2. If you were in Jerry's shoes, would you start looking for a new position outside of your current Company? Why or why not?

3. Should an employee show loyalty to the company that paid most of his or her way through and educational program, in this case an MBA program? Why or why not?

4. What does the company owe Jerry? Why or why not?

5. If you were Jerry's Manager or the Manager of an employee that you promised him or her a promotion upon completion of his or her educational program, and you didn't follow through on that promise, how would you explain your decision to Jerry or other employee on not following through on your promise?

6. Should any Manager or any individual in a Management position make any promise to any of their employees? Why or why not?

Case #5

Is New Job Worth Relocating For?

Maverick (Mav) is a Public Relations Representative I at a small family-run company in Alabama, with annual revenue of $10 million, with an average profit margin of $5 million or 50%. Mav earned a job offer upon completing his internship at the same company. Born and raised in the suburbs of Chicago, Illinois, Mav did not want to attend a college or university near home like many of his high school friends were preparing for. Mav felt like he wanted the challenge of meeting new friends and adapting to life outside of Chicago. The decision to leave his friends and family was emboldened since Mav was one of the Top High School Football recruits at the receiver position. He had full ride football scholarship offers to attend several of the top colleges in the United States including Ohio State, University of Michigan, Clemson University, The University of Oklahoma and The University of

Alabama. Again, Mav could have easily stayed in his home state of Illinois and attended Northwestern University or the University of Illinois. By Mav treating his studies in high school seriously unlike some of his classmates, Mav knew that making the National Football League (NFL) was not automatic and that someday using his intellectual ability would be just as important as his athletic ability to earn a living for him and his future family.

Coming off of another NCAA Division I National Championship, The University of Alabama did not have to do much in the way of recruiting or selling their football program AND their success in job placement upon graduation to potential students and student-athletes. Through much research and consideration, Mav felt blessed and honored to be considered by so many great colleges and universities to continue his athletic and academic career. In the end, Mav ended up choosing The University of Alabama for the next chapter of his life. Mav had a great 4 years with The University of Alabama, who also enjoyed continued success and their winning tradition on the gridiron with securing NCAA Division I National Championships in 3 of Mav's 4 years. The crescendo coming for Mav during the Southeastern Conference (SEC) championship game during the 3rd quarter of his senior year. It started with Mav catching a 20-yard pass on a slant route from his quarterback, securing the football and turning up field with nothing but green grass between him and his 2nd touchdown of the game. However, unfortunately after Mav crossed the plain of the goal line, indeed scoring his second touchdown of the game, Mav heard a loud pop coming from his left leg, and collapsed to the turf of the end zone in excruciating pain. He couldn't help but think of all his past and present teammates that heard that sound, which ultimately sounded the end of their playing days due to the severity of the injury. So inevitably Mav couldn't help but think that this injury would end his playing days at The University of Alabama and seriously jeopardize his chances to showcase his athletic abilities at the NFL Combine and subsequent draft. As intuition would have it, Mav was correct in his future vision and being heartbroken couldn't even begin to describe how he was feeling on the inside as he lay in the endzone being attended to by the on-site medical staff. Mav was hurting not only on the outside physically but inside as well. Luckily Mav's earlier intuition during the selection of his what college/university he would attend was not only based on what he could do on the football field, but also in the classroom. The decision of which college/university to attend came full circle because now it was going to be Mav's academic record that was going to heavily influence his future career success, which now had eliminated playing NFL football from the equation.

Mav graduated from The University of Alabama with a 3.67 grade point average and with a wealth of leadership experience gained as one of the captains of his football team along with leading group class projects regardless of whether the project was small based on a Case Study in the course textbook or a large project that concluded with giving a local business fact based suggestions for near term and long term success in a composed professional like presentation. The past 5 years has encompassed Mav now having gained valuable real-world experience at Company A, an institution that is world known as being quite a bit responsible for the United States of America landing on the moon. Company A is and has been a great company both for the country and for their workforce. However, it is at this point that Mav didn't think he was moving up the corporate ladder fast enough, especially since 3 of his colleagues, colleagues that were brought in to Company A at the same time as Mav, had each been promoted. Mav was at a crossroad, but wanted to be proactive in his career and so he started looking for job opportunities outside of Company A. About a month after Mav began researching & applying to outside job opportunities, he was contacted by a company, Company B with their World headquarters near Chicago, Mav's hometown, to interview for the Public Relations Manager position he had applied to. On the Friday following the first communication with the Company B, Mav found himself taking a flight from Tuscaloosa, Alabama to Chicago, Illinois for an on-site in person interview. The interview came and went without a hitch, since Mav had read The House of You: 5 Workforce Preparation Tips for a Successful Career. He even felt as though he had even aced the interview, a feeling that Mav never felt before. Upon landing in Tuscaloosa, Alabama Mav returned to prepare for another day of work with Company A the next day. Not even a week had passed since the on-site interview with the Chicago based firm and Mav's cell phone started to ring just as he stepped into the employee cafeteria for lunch; It was the Human Resources Manager at Company B, and she wanted to extend Mav a verbal offer, contingent on background check, reference check, work history check and drug test, for the Public Relations Manager position he interviewed for.

Answer the Following Questions About the Case:

1. Should Mav stay at Company A out, or should he leave Company A and move cross-country to begin working at Company B, which is also closer to his hometown?

2. Do you have all of the information you need to make a fact-based decision about the case? If not, what information or data would be helpful in guiding your decision one way or another on what Mav should do?

Additional Information About the Case:

Mav is currently making a base salary gross (before any taxes or any voluntary deductions, such as health insurance, 401 (k), etc.)) of $60,00 with Company A, paid to him on a bi-weekly basis (every 2 weeks), with a 10% annual variable bonus, 3 weeks of paid time off per calendar year, a 401 (k) match by Company A of 100% for the first 6% payroll deducted by Mav, with a commute time of 5 minutes each way and a girlfriend he has been seeing steadily for 3 years, whose hometown is Tuscaloosa, Alabama and has no intention of leaving the area.

Mav is being offered by Company B a base salary gross (before any taxes or any voluntary deductions, such as health insurance, 401 (k), etc.)) of $75,00, also paid to him on a bi-weekly basis (every 2 weeks), with a 5% annual variable bonus, 2 weeks of paid time off per calendar year, a 401 (k) match by Company A of 100% for the first 2% payroll deducted by Mav, with a commute time of 30 minutes each way by train. Mav would now have to start a long-distance relationship with his girlfriend of 3 years, that is if she wants to continue the relationship.

For the next questions below, include the additional information above to help guide your decision making:

1. If Mav chooses Company B, what would his breakeven net income need to be by month and for a full 12 months if his rent would be $1,100/month, cell phone of $85/month, renter's insurance of $300/year, groceries of $200/month, health insurance of $120/month, 401 (k) contributions of 15%, water bill of $15/month, electricity bill of $100/ month, miscellaneous of $150/month?

2. Would you stay in Tuscaloosa and at Company A even if you were unhappy if you were in a relationship with your significant other for 3 years and they didn't want to move with you or be in a long-distance relationship?

3. If the expenses in question #1 above were half if Mav stayed at Company A, do you think that would make a difference? Why or why not?

CONCLUSION

The content found throughout THE HOUSE OF YOU has been constructed from the last fifteen years of my life, which includes my educational and professional experience. As an individual, I strongly feel that it is important to give back to others through whichever means you have at your disposal. Giving back does not always entail money, which is something that I have learned over the years. Giving back can take the form of your time and energy, such as volunteering at a soup kitchen or donating clothes that do not fit anymore to those less fortunate.

Since I had someone to coach me along the process when I was in your shoes, THE HOUSE OF YOU was a project I wanted to do because it is important for me to help students or anyone who wants to put themselves in the best position possible to succeed in this hyper-competitive job market. I am self-taught through education, professional experience, and trial and error. While this book is not a foolproof system to land the most lucrative position at the most prestigious company, it will set you up for success more often than not. I mention throughout THE HOUSE OF YOU that there are areas that you can control and areas outside of your control. That statement could not be truer.

It is easy to "what if" a situation or circumstances as it happens until you become so stressed that only after a given situation has a form of closure, such as after an interview, whether or not you receive a job offer, do you realize you have spent time and energy concerned over things that are outside of your control. What THE

HOUSE OF YOU aims to provide to you are areas that you can control and should focus on, while also bringing to light those areas that are out of your control and should not be focused on.

Just as at the end of each semester I wish my students all the best in their future classes and professional careers, I want to wish you all the best in your professional career, whichever path you take, and I hope that THE HOUSE OF YOU has refreshed and/or given you a few new tools for your tool belt for constructing THE HOUSE OF YOU.

For more information, please go to https://www.thehouseofyou.com to join the career preparation following.

Made in the USA
Lexington, KY
18 August 2019